Jackie Newgent, RDN, CDN

THE all-natural
DIABETES COOKBOOK 2nd edition

The Whole Food Approach to Great Taste and Healthy Eating

American
Diabetes
Association®

Director, Book Publishing, Abe Ogden; *Managing Editor,* Greg Guthrie; *Acquisitions Editor,* Victor Van Beuren; *Project Manager,* Boldface LLC; *Production Manager and Composition,* Melissa Sprott; *Cover Design,* Jenn French Designs, LLC; *Photography,* Tara Donne Photography; *Printer,* Versa Press.

Printed in the United States of America
1 3 5 7 9 10 8 6 4 2

The suggestions and information contained in this publication are generally consistent with the *Standards of Medical Care in Diabetes* and other policies of the American Diabetes Association, but they do not represent the policy or position of the Association or any of its boards or committees. Reasonable steps have been taken to ensure the accuracy of the information presented. However, the American Diabetes Association cannot ensure the safety or efficacy of any product or service described in this publication. Individuals are advised to consult a physician or other appropriate health care professional before undertaking any diet or exercise program or taking any medication referred to in this publication. Professionals must use and apply their own professional judgment, experience, and training and should not rely solely on the information contained in this publication before prescribing any diet, exercise, or medication. The American Diabetes Association—its officers, directors, employees, volunteers, and members—assumes no responsibility or liability for personal or other injury, loss, or damage that may result from the suggestions or information in this publication.

♾ The paper in this publication meets the requirements of the ANSI Standard Z39.48-1992 (permanence of paper).

American Diabetes Association titles may be purchased for business or promotional use or for special sales. To purchase more than 50 copies of this book at a discount, or for custom editions of this book with your logo, contact the American Diabetes Association at the address below or at booksales@diabetes.org.

American Diabetes Association
1701 North Beauregard Street
Alexandria, Virginia 22311

DOI: 10.2337/9781580405454

Library of Congress Cataloging-in-Publication Data

Newgent, Jackie.
  The all-natural diabetes cookbook : the whole food approach to great taste and healthy eating / Jackie Newgent, RDN, CDN. -- 2nd edition.
     pages cm
  Includes bibliographical references and index.
  ISBN 978-1-58040-545-4 (alk. paper)
  1. Diabetes--Diet therapy--Recipes. 2. Cooking (Natural foods) I. American Diabetes Association II. Title.
  RC662.N494 2015
  641.5'6314--dc23
                        2014043347

For my father, to help manage your diabetes.

For my nephews, to help keep you healthy.

Contents

Acknowledgments

I have many people to thank for their generous time, energy, and support of this project—and for helping me fully pursue my passion for great taste and healthy eating.

I'm grateful to my:

- late mother, for all she taught me about the importance and love of high-quality foods.

- father, the true inspiration for this cookbook.

- thoughtful sister, Dr. Rebecca Newgent, for her help in retesting several of the book's recipes; my generous brother, Jim Newgent, for his constant support; and my sister-in-law, Sandi Newgent, for allowing me to test recipes out on her and my nephews, Aiden and Rhyus.

- dear friends, for being so supportive and understanding when I made my cookbook a priority.

- interns, Maeve Guidera, Lea Loveland, Sheila Mulhern, and Tida Pradith, for their smart culinary nutrition insights.

- agent, Beth Shepard, for cheerfully guiding my career with her intuition and wisdom.

- creative team, Tara Donne, Carrie Purcell, Chelsie Craig, Monica Pierini, Kira Corbin, and Alex Broderick, for the amazing photography, food styling, and prop styling in this book.

- editors and the dedicated behind-the-scenes talent at the American Diabetes Association, including Abe Ogden, Greg Guthrie, and Lauren Wilson.

Thank you so much to all!

Introduction

When it comes to eating right, I find it's so important for food to be tasty, so that you'll want to keep eating well for a lifetime. Luckily, you don't need to give up deliciousness to eat better. *The All-Natural Diabetes Cookbook, 2nd Edition* provides everyday favorites for every taste, made healthy with the addition of whole food nutrition and flavor, not subtraction of scrumptiousness.

There's nothing artificial here! You won't find overly processed foods in this cookbook. But you will find great-tasting ingredients in just the right quantities and cooking techniques that maximize their flavor and wholesomeness. With the overriding food philosophy of "fresh is best," I'll show you how to use 100% real foods in your cooking: plenty of seasonal fresh vegetables, fruits, and herbs, as well as whole grains, beans, healthful fats, and fresh poultry, fish, and lean meat. Your job is simply to choose the most natural ingredients you can. And aim to plan meals that are more plant centered than meat focused. Then set aside a little time to enjoy the art of cooking and savor your results!

Simplicity is key in *The All-Natural Diabetes Cookbook, 2nd Edition*. I realize that you probably don't have the time or desire to spend hours in the kitchen. "All-natural" convenience foods, like prepackaged salad greens or canned beans, help save time.

You'll find recipes here for every eating style. It is the position of the American Diabetes Association that there is not a "one-size-fits-all" eating pattern for individuals with diabetes. Whichever pattern you follow, there are plenty of carb-conscious meal and snack choices for you—from breakfast to dessert—in this cookbook. Complete nutritional facts accompany the recipes to help you easily fit each dish into an individualized, diabetes-friendly meal plan.

The bottom line: Using the freshest, least-processed foods provides a way for people with diabetes (and their families) to eat healthfully, naturally, and deliciously—for a lifetime!

INGREDIENT HIGHLIGHTS

Here's an overview of the ingredients you'll find in this cookbook:

- **Whole foods:** Eating "real" is the basis for this cookbook. That means no ingredient is overly processed or artificial in any way. Reduced-fat and other nutrient-modified foods are kept to a minimum. They're included only when they contain nothing artificial and when the dish's overall flavor appeal isn't adversely affected by their use.

- **Mediterranean-style approach:** A Mediterranean diet seems to have beneficial effects for people with, or those who are at risk for, diabetes; it may slow diabetes progression! The consumption of plant foods overall is encouraged. Foods with "good" fats, such as extra-virgin olive oil, avocados, and nuts are celebrated, not shunned. Plus, all recipes in this book have zero grams of trans fat.

- **Rich ingredients:** Butter and full-flavored regular cheeses, for instance, are used in just-right amounts when needed to make a dish more flavorful while still meeting healthful nutritional guidelines. This is based on the philosophy that enjoyment is an important part of a long-term approach to a healthful, diabetes-friendly lifestyle.

- **Organic foods:** To make these recipes accessible for everyone, I don't label the majority of ingredients in the recipe lists as "organic." However, I do encourage the purchase of organic foods when possible. They're produced without using most conventional pesticides and without fertilizers made with synthetic ingredients. They're free of genetically modified organisms (GMOs). In some cases, they may be more nutrient-rich than their conventional counterparts. You can find organic versions of most foods and beverages these days.

- **Eco-friendly poultry and meat:** Poultry and meat are used in petite portions in this cookbook. Enjoying smaller meat and poultry portions is good for overall health as well as the environment. When ham or bacon is listed, the uncured version is recommended. Beyond that, everything is kept natural. It's your choice to determine other quality features that are important to you and your family. For instance, choose grass-fed beef or lamb; their diet throughout their lifespan is mainly grass. Select organic chicken, turkey, pork, beef, and lamb, when possible; they're from animals that aren't given antibiotics. If you're buying conventional meat or poultry, at minimum make sure it's raised without antibiotics. This may ultimately help reduce the occurrence of antibiotic-resistant bacteria (also known as "superbugs").

Sustainable seafood: The fish and shellfish selected for the recipes in this cookbook are considered in abundant supply and caught (or farmed) in an eco-friendly manner. (Hint: For an updated list of the most eco-friendly fish and shellfish, see the recommendations of the Seafood Watch program at the Monterey Bay Aquarium by visiting seafoodwatch.org.)

Whole grains: Whole grains, like brown rice and farro, and whole-grain foods, like whole-wheat pasta, whole-wheat pastry flour, and whole-grain bread, are exclusively used instead of their refined counterparts, such as white rice, all-purpose flour, or white bread. For bread products, you can take them a step further and choose sprouted whole-grain versions, when available. These versions may have greater nutritional benefits. If you're not able to eat wheat, various whole-grain and bean products, like garbanzo bean flour and edamame noodles, are now available. Look for other new, wholesome varieties of whole-grain products. Check their packaging for suggestions on using them in place of traditional versions.

Beans: To provide protein and satisfaction in place of meat, beans are the star of several of these recipes. They're also smartly used to create creaminess in a salad dressing and to extend meat. Canned beans help save time. Including beans in your meal routine is one of the easiest ways to boost soluble fiber intake, too.

Nonstarchy Vegetables: Nonstarchy vegetables are utilized liberally in this book to promote more of a plant-centered approach to eating—and they go way beyond their traditional role in side dishes or salads. Some vegetables become entrées, such as a cauliflower "steak." And mushrooms are blended into some meatier recipes to boost savoriness while reducing the total meat amounts without shrinking overall portion size. However, it's up to you to fit plentiful amounts of these vegetables into your meals. A good rule of thumb is to fill half of your plate with nonstarchy vegetables, whether grilled, steamed, roasted, microwave-baked, or raw. Try to enjoy a colorful array throughout the day—including red, blue/purple, green, white, and yellow/orange vegetables—since each color group provides distinctive health benefits. In your meals, this might translate to tomatoes, eggplant, spinach, onions, and/or carrots.

Fruits and real fruit products: Fresh fruit, pure fruit juice, unsweetened fruit sauces, and 100% fruit spreads are used in these recipes to provide sweetness in a good-for-you way. Whole fruits are emphasized. Unsweetened applesauce is used to provide sweetness in place of sugar, when possible. Bananas are used in some desserts in place of ingredients with added sugar, such as ice cream.

Sugar: Though kept to a minimum, naturally derived sugar is used in select recipes for its baking properties or to boost deliciousness, since people with diabetes can enjoy a small amount of sweets when they properly plan for them. Specifically, the recipes include turbinado or coconut palm sugar, honey, coconut nectar, or pure maple syrup; all are less processed than white sugar. The coconut palm sugar and coconut nectar can be your best bets for blood glucose management.

No artificial sweeteners: To keep recipes as natural and tasty as possible, artificial sweeteners are not used. However, if you need to be especially restrictive with carbohydrate or overall calorie intake, you can replace some or all of the sugar or honey in a recipe with a naturally-derived, zero-calorie sweetener, such as stevia-based or monk fruit–based sweetener. Use the guidelines provided on sweetener packaging for advice on adjusting these recipes.

Herbs and spices: Fresh herbs are utilized as integral ingredients in this cookbook, not as afterthoughts or just for garnish. (Hint: They count as part of your vegetable intake!) Spices are used regularly in these dishes to boost aroma, flavor, and antioxidants. Don't be shy with them!

Sea salt: These recipes are designed to taste great, so salt is not left out. But it is kept to a moderate level. Keep in mind that your body does have a minimum need for sodium. So if you start with fresh ingredients, as most of the recipes in this book do, you'll be eating mainly foods that have little to no sodium naturally. Shaking a bit of salt onto these foods can bring out full flavors and actually make you want to keep eating the healthful dishes. To avoid oversalting, please note that a "pinch" of salt (or any spice) in this cookbook is equivalent to 1/16 teaspoon. If you prefer or need to restrict sodium, you can absolutely use less or none of the suggested amount. In any case, I advise using sea salt as it has a taste I prefer over regular iodized table salt.

BONUS FEATURES

You'll notice some bonus features throughout the recipes, too. There are easy-to-identify recipe symbols used throughout the cookbook to assure there's something to fit everyone's needs.

 is for quickest-to-fix dishes; they generally require 20 minutes or less to prepare—from start to finish.

 means the recipe is vegetarian—eggs and dairy may be included. Some recipes are suitable for vegans, too—no animal products included.

Each recipe also has tips on choosing ingredients, cooking techniques, timesaving tricks, or party planning advice. These tips include:

- 🌿 FRESH FACT
- 🌿 FOOD FLAIR
- 🌿 FAST FIX
- 🌿 MORE THAN FOUR?

WHAT'S NATURAL?

There's currently no official, standardized definition for the term "natural" that applies to all foods and beverages. The U.S. Food and Drug Administration (FDA) does not have an established formal definition. The U.S. Department of Agriculture (USDA) released a draft guidance in 2013 stating that "non-synthetic (natural)" is a substance that is derived from mineral, plant, or animal matter and does not undergo a synthetic process. Additionally, more than half of the states in the U.S. have introduced legislation or ballot initiatives requiring the labeling of genetically modified organisms (GMOs), in some instances providing a statutory definition for "natural." So, if we're lucky, standards may soon come to help clarify any confusion with this terminology.

On the other hand, the USDA does have a standardized definition of "natural" as it applies specifically to meat, poultry, and egg products: they can only be "natural" if they contain no artificial ingredients or added colors and are only minimally processed. Minimal processing means that the product was processed in a way that does not fundamentally alter it. While we wait for other products to be defined similarly, don't be misled by "natural" marketing gimmicks.

My own goals in writing this book are that ingredients follow these standards:

- 🌿 No artificial or synthetic ingredients, flavors, or colors of any kind (including no "bleached" ingredients)
- 🌿 No overly processed foods (Note: meat, poultry, or egg products need to meet the USDA's definition of "natural")
- 🌿 No GMOs (thorough label reading is important to assure non-GMO options are selected)
- 🌿 No hydrogenated fats and zero grams of trans fat
- 🌿 No swordfish, shark, tilefish, king mackerel, or other fish with a high mercury content

In many instances, it will be your prerogative to make smart selections when shopping and to assure these goals are met whenever you can. If you're in doubt about whether a product meets the criteria above, read the food label carefully and choose wisely. For instance, instead of just buying any bottle of ketchup, read the ingredient list first. If it contains corn syrup, it'll generally have GMOs. You'll then ideally want to pick a different brand of ketchup. If you're still in doubt, go organic when possible.

WHAT'S ORGANIC?

With all of the label lingo that can appear on food packaging, it can be confusing to know which products are the best options for you. Luckily, there is one word—"organic"—that is a standardized term; therefore, you'll know the true story behind what you're getting when you buy organic. Organic food is produced by farmers who emphasize the use of renewable resources and the conservation of soil and water to enhance environmental quality. Organic crops are produced without using irradiation, sewage sludge, synthetic fertilizers, prohibited pesticides, or GMOs. Organic livestock is produced without using antibiotics or growth hormones; the animals are fed 100% organic feed, are provided with access to the outdoors, and are raised to meet animal health and welfare standards. Organic multi-ingredients have 95% or more certified organic content.

How do you know if something is organic? Look for the word "organic" and the USDA Organic seal on packages of meat, cartons of milk and eggs, cheese, fresh produce, and other single-ingredient foods. Or you might see a sign above organic produce sections. Alternatively, look for the price look-up (PLU) sticker on organic produce; a five-digit code beginning with the number "9" is an indicator that the item is organic. For foods with more than one ingredient, you'll probably see a statement noting the percentages of organic ingredients included, such as "made with at least 70% organic ingredients."

The USDA Organic seal on food labels tells you that a product is certified as either 100% organic or 95–100% organic. Though organic foods can be more costly than conventionally produced foods, I find them worth any added expense. You'll notice that I specifically call for a few selected ingredients in this cookbook to be organic. That's a good place to start. Later, try adding organic meat . . . organic produce can be next. (See "Beware of the Dirty Dozen" on page 8.) Set a personal goal to make half of your food and beverage choices organic—or whatever is manageable for you. Your body and taste buds will thank you.

The products in *The All-Natural Diabetes Cookbook, 2nd Edition* that I've labeled as organic in the ingredient lists are the following:

- major sources of soybeans, including edamame, tofu, tempeh, miso, and soy milk
- mayonnaise
- corn and corn products, including corn tortillas and tortilla chips
- low-fat sour cream
- turkey bacon
- wine

This list may seem a bit unusual, but there is logic behind it. The majority of the soybeans and corn grown in the U.S. are genetically modified. That's the rationale behind my labeling the products from these two categories as organic in this book. Organically grown soybeans and corn will be GMO-free. (See "A Note about GMOs.") The most popular commercially produced mayonnaises on the market are made with either soybean or canola oil. Canola is a crop that is mainly genetically modified, too. (That's also why I simply chose not to include canola oil in this cookbook.) I've included low-fat sour cream on the organic list for two reasons: to provide the best flavor and because other readily available low-fat versions of sour cream may contain ingredients like dried corn syrup, modified food starch, and artificial color. Choosing the organic variety of turkey bacon is the best way to assure it'll be free of the preservative sodium nitrite. Finally, wine made this organic list because when it's certified organic in the U.S., it will be free of added sulfites, a synthetic food additive used as a preservative. There's also a personal reason; I have a true sulfite allergy and can only sip on (or cook with) no-sulfite-added wines!

A Note about GMOs

So what's all the fuss about GMOs? "GMOs," or "genetically modified organisms," are plants or animals created basically by merging DNA from different species in a way that could not occur in nature or by traditional crossbreeding techniques. Unfortunately, there's still not a significant enough body of research in this arena to form firm and sweeping conclusions on the benefits or harms of this use of biotechnology.

However, what we do know is that GMO seeds have not been shown to absolutely increase crop yields and, in some cases, may result in lower yields than conventional counterparts. There has been an increase in weed resistance due to GMO seeds, which makes crop production more challenging. Herbicide use on GMO corn is on the rise, too. What's more, the potential issues of consuming genetically modified foods may include allergenic effects and negatively impacted nutritional value.

With that in mind, I suggest these three key ways to avoid GMOs: (1) Go organic when possible, since the USDA National Organic Standards do not allow GMOs; (2) look for the Non-GMO Project Verified seal on food packages; or (3) if you're a Whole Foods Market shopper, choose 365 Everyday Value brand food products, since all plant-derived ingredients in these products are sourced to avoid GMOs.

Altogether, GMOs raise a lot of questions for me because my philosophy is this: The further we stray from food produced the way nature intended, the more unintended consequences may result. I'm quite concerned about the long-term consumption of genetically modified foods on future health. My hope is that, at minimum, all foods will be required to be labeled if they contain GMOs. I'm for labeling, so we can all make informed choices. In the meantime, I choose to err on the side of caution...and nature.

NATURAL VS. ORGANIC

"Natural" and "organic" aren't the same thing. Organic refers to an agricultural growing method, not a health claim. Organic food differs from conventionally produced food in how it's grown, handled, and processed, but that doesn't mean it's always preservative-free or "all-natural." Natural products ideally are free of added chemicals and preservatives, are minimally processed, and may have organic ingredients.

The goal is to eat as naturally as possible. This will help assure that your body is getting the nutrients it needs, not the chemicals it doesn't. Read all food labels carefully. When shopping for natural foods, don't automatically assume that you need to head to a health food store. The best-tasting products may come from small, local farmers who grow produce and raise animals organically. Shop at nearby farmers' markets regularly. You'll have the highest-quality ingredients at fair prices and wonderfully fresh, seasonal fruits, vegetables, herbs, meats, cheeses, and more.

Buy natural foods whenever you can. Buy organic foods selectively and whenever you can afford them. And we'll all have more sustainable communities and ideally more delicious, nutritious food on our plates.

Beware of the Dirty Dozen

The USDA doesn't claim that organically produced food is more nutritious or safer than conventionally produced food. However, according to the Environmental Working Group (EWG), it's best to go organic when buying certain fruits and vegetables, as research finds it can reduce your exposure to chemicals found in and on conventionally produced food.

The EWG has a list of the "dirty dozen," which catalogues produce with the most pesticide residues. According to EWG's 2015 Shopper's Guide to Pesticides in Produce, you should try to choose organic when buying these 12 fresh fruits or vegetables: apples, peaches, nectarines, strawberries, grapes, celery, spinach, sweet bell peppers, cucumbers, cherry tomatoes, imported snap peas, and potatoes. If you want to go a step further, consider purchasing organic hot peppers or kale/collard greens, too. Since this list is updated annually, visit ewg.org each year for the latest information.

ACHIEVING HIGH-FLAVOR DISHES NATURALLY

One of the missing components in many diabetes cookbooks is great flavor. Luckily, that's the highlight of *The All-Natural Diabetes Cookbook, 2nd Edition*. Below are 22 techniques that will help you love your food. Most of these tips are already incorporated into this cookbook, but use these suggestions at home to give your own recipes a high-flavor makeover.

1. **Be liberal with herbs.** Herbs are in the vegetable category, after all. Plus, fresh herbs can add fragrance and flavor along with antioxidants to a finished dish. For the freshest, fullest flavor, add fresh herbs toward the end of the cooking process or just before serving a dish. Tip: Save money by growing your own herb garden outdoors or in a windowsill.

2. **Spice it up.** Kick up flavors one spice at a time. Begin by adding 1/4 teaspoon of your spice of choice per recipe—and increase it from there. You may find, too, that you'll use a little less salt when you sprinkle a savory dish with spices first. Also, consider adding a dash of a "sweet spice," like cinnamon or nutmeg, to either sweet or savory dishes for a hint of sweetness without adding sugar.

3. **Marry in marinade.** Marinating ingredients to be cooked can help boost nutrition, tenderness, and taste. If you're marinating at room temperature, marinate for no more than two hours. Ideally, you should marinate foods in a covered container in the refrigerator. Try marinating poultry breasts in buttermilk or yogurt; it creates succulence.

4. **Go nuts—and seeds.** Nuts and seeds add rich flavor, texture, visual appeal, and, well, nuttiness. Vary the interest further by choosing sliced, chopped, and/or whole varieties. Go for even more flavor by pan-toasting raw nuts and seeds first. You can scatter roasted sunflower seeds or toasted almonds onto nearly any salad. Use pistachios for a green effect.

5. **Get saucy with it.** Even when recipes don't call for it, plop in a few drops of a full-flavored sauce. It heightens flavor—and you might be able to cut out or reduce added salt. Sprinkle a few drops of worcestershire, hot pepper, or naturally brewed soy sauce into low-sodium soups and stews.

6. **Drizzle and sizzle.** Experiment with aromatic oils, like truffle, toasted sesame, hot chile, or garlic- or herb-infused extra-virgin olive oil. A little healthful fat can go a long way in added flair. Try these swaps for butter: Scramble eggs in herb-infused oil, drizzle organic popcorn with truffle oil, or sauté carrots in toasted sesame oil.

7. **Say "cheese, please."** Top healthful dishes with high-flavored, high-fat ingredients, such as cheese. When it's so flavorful, very little is needed, making it easy to create a dish that's still healthful—and more enjoyable. When selecting cheese, always be sure it's real cheese (not a pasteurized processed cheese food!) and often pick one of the three S's: sharp, smoky, or stinky. Sprinkle an ordinary calorie-friendly salad with crumbled blue cheese or naturally smoked mozzarella; it'll become rather extraordinary.

8. **Splash with acid.** Balance and uplift flavors with citrus juices, vinegars, or wines. Try matching by color. Lemon pairs well with fish, orange with chicken, and red wine with beef. Add a few splashes of aged balsamic or red wine vinegar into bottled spaghetti sauce when simmering or to fresh tomato slices when serving.

9. **Get zesty.** If you plan to use lemon, lime, or orange juice in a recipe, grate the citrus peel first. The grated zest can add extra zing and color to your meals (for virtually no calories), even if a recipe doesn't call for its use. Lemon zest can add the essence of saltiness, which may help you add less salt to your cuisine.

10. **Reduce and seduce.** Reductions magnify flavor and can create thickness for a more seductive mouth feel. Simmer a creamy, low-sodium, low-calorie carrot, butternut squash, or other veggie soup until extra thick. Ladle it onto your meal as a sauce instead of serving it as a soup.

11. **Grill with flair.** Charcoal grilling is a popular cooking technique. It can be healthful since no added fat is required. Make it more flavorful by adding woods, herbs, and spices to the coals. Grill boneless, skinless chicken breasts over aromatic woods, such as mesquite. Add rosemary twigs or cinnamon sticks, too.

12. **Brown it.** The browning of vegetables, for example, is called caramelization. Besides adding rich color, it creates savory sweetness. Caramelize onions and serve on top of turkey or veggie burgers as a condiment, stir into steamed brown rice for intrigue, or add to plain broth to make a simple onion soup.

13. **Boost the beans.** Beans provide beneficial fiber, nutrient richness, and texture to meals. They're versatile, too. Plop canned beans into pasta sauce, soups, stews, salads, and stir-fry dishes. Use bean dips, like hummus, as a lovely sandwich spread. Mash cooked black beans and serve as a "bed" for entrées, such as roast pork loin. (If you purchase canned beans, there's no need to rinse them after draining—this can remove a small amount of nutrients. However, if you need to watch your sodium intake, do rinse canned beans that contain added salt—this can reduce the sodium content of the beans by 40%!)

14. **Be big with veggies.** Along with nutritional goodness, vegetables add texture, visual appeal, and natural savoriness (and sometimes slight sweetness) to meals. Don't hunt for perfection. Sometimes the most delicious vegetables are those that appear a little odd or that still have a little dirt on them, which is the way nature intended. Just clean and love these vegetables like any others. Enjoy veggies as entrées more often. Pile sandwiches high with raw or grilled veggies. Sneak in vegetables, too, by using low-sodium vegetable or tomato juice for the preparation of whole-wheat couscous, bulgur wheat, or brown rice.

15. **Flavor with fruit.** Fruits add texture, visual appeal, and natural sweetness—plus antioxidant nutrition. If a fruit is out of season, use frozen fruit since it's healthful, too. Serve salad topped with sliced pears or apples. Purée berries or other fruits with equal parts oil and vinegar to make a zippy fruit vinaigrette. Incorporate unsweetened apple butter or apple-

sauce into baked good recipes as the "sugar" of choice. Make a refreshing salsa with diced peaches, onion, red bell pepper, and mint; serve with grilled fish or chicken.

16. **Opt for whole grains.** Don't just eat whole grains and whole-grain food products because you know they provide fiber and plenty of other good-for-you nutrients. Choose them because they're more interesting on the plate and your palate than their traditional white counterparts. Try various brands and varieties of whole-grain pasta, including those containing quinoa flour. Though technically a seed, quinoa is considered a "supergrain." And it doesn't contain wheat, so it's a smart gluten-free pick. Basically, use whole-grain products just like you would the refined versions; just check cooking times on package labels as they may differ.

17. **Make it hot, hot, hot.** A touch of "heat" takes flavor appeal to the next level. It adds more enjoyment to foods—especially those that are low in fat or sodium. Top grilled fish or lean poultry or meat with spicy salsas. Purée jalapeño pepper into hummus or other bean dips. Or sprinkle hot sauce wherever you like; it can brighten the flavors of soups and most other savory foods. Even if you don't like spicy foods, just a drop or two of hot sauce can create flavor depth without adding notable "heat."

18. **Whip it good.** Whipping up organic silken tofu in a blender creates a velvety smooth flavor carrier and volume extender for sauces, salad dressings, dips, smoothies, and more. While blending, add other flavorful ingredients, such as balsamic vinegar and fresh basil, and use as a sandwich condiment.

19. **Eat tea.** Brew black, green, white, or herbal tea and use in vinaigrettes or as a poaching or other cooking liquid. It can add unique flavor and, in some instances, color, especially when used in place of plain ol' water. Use tea as the main ingredient in a marinade to help chicken breasts develop a golden color. Try my favorite tea for cooking: jasmine green tea.

20. **Up the umami.** Umami is considered the fifth taste. It adds scrumptious savoriness to foods. Be sure to stock your kitchen with naturally rich, high-umami foods—and be sure to use them (see "Upping Umami...Naturally" on page 12).

21. **Allow overnight mingling.** Cooking in advance and refrigerating overnight allows flavors to mingle in many mixed dishes. And it saves time on the day you plan to serve the food. Leftovers can be lovable, too. Make dips, creamy chicken salads, or grain-based salads the day before you plan to eat them.

22. **Choose water wisely**. If you don't like the taste of your tap water, then consider whether or not you really want to cook with water straight from your kitchen faucet. The quality of every ingredient used in your cuisine, including water, makes an impact on overall taste enjoyment. Consider using filtered water for your cooking, not just for your drinking. You don't need to install a complex water filtration system if you don't already have that in place. Pitcher-style filtered water will do. That's what I use!

Upping Umami...Naturally

Umami is one of the five basic tastes (the others are sweet, salty, sour, and bitter). Umami is derived from the Japanese words *umai*, which means "delicious," and *mi*, which means "essence." Many people describe its taste as "meaty" or "savory." By including high-umami ingredients in healthful cooking, you'll naturally be adding savory satisfaction. Stock your kitchen pantry, fridge, or freezer with these umami-rich foods. Be sure to pick natural varieties of these foods, too.

- Aged balsamic vinegar
- Aged cheeses, including blue and parmigiano-reggiano cheese
- Beef (but keep portions petite!)
- Black beans
- Broth/stock, chicken and beef (low-sodium)
- Eggs
- Mushrooms, fresh and dried, such as morel, shiitake, and portobello
- Peas, fresh or frozen
- Red wine, preferably organic
- Sea vegetables (seaweeds)
- Seeds and nuts, including sunflower seeds and almonds
- Sauces, like worcestershire, black bean, soy, and Asian fish sauces
- Shellfish and dark-fleshed fish, including salmon and anchovies
- Soybean products, including organic miso and organic tofu
- Tomatoes and tomato products
- Truffle oil

---

33 NATURAL, NO-FUSS COOKING AND BAKING TIPS

Some people are worried that cooking more healthfully will take more time. It doesn't have to! Most recipes in *The All-Natural Diabetes Cookbook, 2nd Edition* are already quick to fix. And here are 33 suggestions that you can use at home to make your own recipes speedier or easier to prepare.

1. **Gather your mise en place** [MEEZ ahn plahs]. This is a French cooking term that means "everything in its place." Measuring or portioning ingredients in advance, and organizing them in the order that you need them, will make your cooking efforts more efficient and enjoyable. It works for me!

2. **Pick nonstick.** While allowing for minimal cooking fat, using nonstick or other stick-resistant cookware can help prevent foods from getting stuck to the pan, making cooking and cleanup less stressful. Pick nonstick skillets that are PFOA-free; they're better for the environment and, ultimately, for you since they don't contain this potentially harmful chemical. Or go with well-seasoned cast iron skillets or grill pans; they work really well for browning foods and little cleanup will be required.

3. **Create nonstick.** Natural oil cooking spray can help prevent sticking during your stovetop cooking. Make your own—you'll need to buy a culinary pump-spray bottle and select the oil, such as grapeseed or extra-virgin olive oil. Use it for all of the recipes in this cookbook

that call for cooking spray. For best results, consider spraying the food, not the pan, when you can. This will result in less sticky buildup. And if you're planning to use the oven, form a "nonstick" surface by baking on unbleached parchment paper rather than directly on a baking sheet.

4. **Skinny-size it.** The skinnier the ingredients to be cooked, the speedier the cooking process. For instance, make paillards—by pounding pieces of poultry, meat, or firm fish until very thin—for quicker sautéing or grilling and more plate coverage. Choose skinny, pencil-like asparagus stalks instead of those as thick as your thumb.

5. **Mix it up.** Create pancake, cookie, muffin, or spice mixes when you have a spare moment, so you'll save time when ready to fix. Create several batches at once, too. All you need to do is combine the main dry ingredients that are called for in the recipes. Make your own pancake mix by measuring flours, baking powder, and salt. Make oatmeal cookie mix by measuring oats, flour, baking powder, and salt. Label, date, and store each mix in a well-sealed jar for weeks.

6. **Freeze for ease.** When fresh fruits, like raspberries, aren't in season, or you don't want to mess with peeling or slicing whole fruit, like mangos, use frozen fruits. They're a nutritious option in place of fresh fruit since they're frozen at their peak of ripeness, nutritional value, and flavor. The same applies to vegetables, like peas or organic corn.

7. **Love your leftovers.** Even when recipes call for freshly prepared ingredients, leftovers will often work perfectly—and be speedier. Chicken salad, for instance, tastes wonderful using roasted chicken leftovers. If the chicken is already seasoned, just adjust other seasonings in the recipe accordingly. Also, a grilled veggie sandwich is delicious when made with vegetables that have been grilled 2 minutes, 2 hours, or 2 days in advance. I call leftover dishes "vintage cuisine" to make them sound more appealing!

8. **Don't kick the can.** Use organic canned beans, tomatoes, or corn to save time. These foods are canned when in-season, at their peak of ripeness, nutritional value, and flavor. When going organic, there's usually just water and sometimes salt or sea salt added to these plant-based foods. So, they're still natural. And organic canned foods can be more nutritious than fresh produce that's out of season or that had to travel hundreds of miles to reach your kitchen table.

9. **Befriend your butcher.** Befriend your fishmonger, too. He or she can cut roasts and steaks "to order" for you. All of the guesswork and trimming time is taken care of for your recipe. It'll cut the need for an extra cutting board at prep time, as well.

10. **Similar-size it.** When ingredients are about the same size, they can be cooked about the same length of time. That's true from cookies to kebabs and poultry to potatoes. One example: if you're roasting baby potatoes, but some aren't baby-sized, cut them into similar-size pieces or halve the largest ones. This'll provide more even—and faster—cooking.

11. **Do it yourself.** Don't spend too much time hunting at the supermarket for specialty ingredients. Make your own versions. For instance, add a few drops of hot pepper sauce to regular dijon mustard to create spicy mustard. Stir a little coconut nectar or honey into regular mustard to create honey mustard. Or try both at once to make spicy honey mustard.

12. **Don't do it yourself.** A growing number of prepackaged, prewashed, presliced, and preportioned food choices are now available. They're ideal when time is of the essence. But be sure to buy those that are natural and without "hidden" ingredients. Prepackaged baby spinach, pregrilled chicken breast pieces, and chopped nuts are all popular time-saving picks.

13. **Use utensils wisely.** Use a chef's knife instead of dirtying a food processor for small chopping tasks. Choose a small ice cream or cookie scoop for forming perfectly sized meatballs. Try a grapefruit spoon for super-easy tomato or melon scooping.

14. **Give in to commercials.** Some major food companies have natural foods. So, don't judge a food just by company name. Foods that are TV commercial stars may be healthful, too. They can help expand the array of choices available to you—and save specialty shopping time.

15. **Fill the fridge.** Many ingredients, parts of recipes, and entire recipes can be made 1, 2, or 3 days in advance. Roast beets, wrap well, and chill; they're recipe-ready any time for the next couple of days. Slice or dice veggies, like bell peppers, onions, and zucchini, up to a day before you need them. Keep them well sealed and chilled. Prepare and refrigerate soups, sauces, and stews uncovered, overnight. Some of the fat solidifies on top when chilled and you can then remove it.

16. **Mix 'n' mingle.** Some foods are actually tastiest when cooked ahead of time and refrigerated overnight. It allows for flavors to mingle—and frees up your time the day you plan to serve the food, which is especially important when party planning. Sauces, spreads, and dips are good examples. It's true of pasta, tuna, and chicken salad, too. Be sure to add any crunchy items, like nuts, just before serving.

17. **Chill out.** Baked goods are generally good candidates for freezing. And when you package them individually, it'll be easier to eat just one serving instead of being tempted by more. So, bake and freeze muffins, cookies, cupcakes, brownie squares, and cake slices. Place one packaged serving on the counter at room temperature in the morning and it'll be ready to enjoy in the evening.

18. **Cheat!** Go ahead and take it easy on yourself when cooking—cheating's not always a bad idea! Grab a rotisserie chicken from the grocery store, remove the skin, and pull the chicken from the bone to use in a quick-cooking recipe. Or simply take a shortcut. When a recipe calls for salsa and a jalapeño pepper, skip the jalapeño and use a spicy salsa instead. If a recipe suggests a mixture of white and dark meat, just use white to save some time—and some calories, too

19. **Let it lie.** Having a lazy, stay-at-home Sunday? If so, take a few minutes and prepare items that can be stored in airtight containers and kept on the counter for the week (or longer). Pan-toast nuts, bake homemade granola, and more.

20. **Marinate in minutes.** Often a marinade is used mostly for flavoring, not tenderizing. When that's the case, use half of it to marinate in minutes, rather than hours. Then use the other half as a basting liquid during cooking or a dipping sauce at the table. Just make sure you never reuse marinade that raw meat, poultry, or fish has been soaking in.

21. **Procrastinate on purpose.** When a recipe seems lengthy, do some of it today and save some of it for tomorrow. Review the recipe first to determine what can be done in advance.

22. **Grill in.** Too cold outside, no gas in the tank, or no desire to mess with charcoal briquettes? Grill inside, not out. There are indoor electric and gas grills, grill pans, and panini-style grills from which to choose. My personal favorite to use, whenever appropriate, is a cast-iron grill pan. I actually use it so much that it stays on my stovetop! Which option you use depends on what you plan to grill. Broiling is another speedy alternative to outdoor grilling.

23. **Cook once; eat twice.** Grain dishes are often tasty served hot or cold. Quinoa or bulgur side dishes are prime examples. Serve them hot the first day, then chill the leftovers. The next day, squirt with fresh lemon juice or splash with vinegar of your choice and serve as a cool side salad. Or, simply make extra of your favorite ingredients, like grilled asparagus or chicken breasts, so they'll be available for use in various recipes over the next couple of days.

24. **Be boring.** Variety isn't always the spice of life. When a recipe calls for four types of beans, three types of bell peppers, or two types of berries, it's often for color variety. But these recipes will still taste good with only one type of bean, bell pepper, or berry. It'll save shopping time, prep time, and maybe money, too.

25. **Thaw while you sleep.** When a recipe calls for a frozen item to be thawed, don't wait until you're preparing the recipe to do so. Zapping it in the microwave can create a partially thawed, partially cooked, partially still-frozen mess. And thawing on the counter is unsafe for many foods. Instead, thaw items overnight in the fridge while you're dreaming. It'll help prevent a potential nightmare at prep time.

26. **Do two (or three) things at once.** Make good use of your time when cooking. Fully review recipes in advance to determine what should be done first, what can wait for last, and what can be done at the same time. Jot the steps down if that helps you. Often while something is cooking, other parts of a recipe or meal can be gathered, measured, and prepped.

27. **Mix up mealtime.** Don't always think of eggs or oatmeal as breakfast foods, or pasta or steak as dinner foods. Mix things up. Eggs are so easy to fix and can be part of an absolutely delicious dinner. Try a fast frittata. Whole-grain pasta can be part of a balanced breakfast for those willing to break out of the traditional meal pattern. Simple whole-grain spaghetti with tomato, basil, and mozzarella for breakfast? Sure!

28. **Fix it your way.** For baked dessert recipes, you need to be pretty precise with measurements. But most other recipes don't usually need to be followed to a tee. Make each recipe your own and have fun in the process. For instance, if you can't find heirloom tomatoes, go with vine-ripened beefsteak tomatoes. If you need to limit salt, don't add all of the salt called for in a recipe—sprinkle with grated lemon zest and boost the spices or herbs instead. If you don't like olives, replace them with sun-dried tomatoes. (Tip: To rehydrate sun-dried tomatoes, simply soak them in simmering low-sodium vegetable broth or water for a few minutes, then drain.)

29. **Think outside the recipe.** A soup can also be a gravy. An appetizer can be a salad. And so on. For example, a creamy chestnut soup is a delicious soup, but it can also be a unique gravy for turkey or mashed potatoes. Serve some beef or chicken satays as appetizers, then dice some of the satay meat and serve in a salad. When one recipe works as two, it saves time and can add intrigue to meals.

30. **Make it a family affair.** Have the entire family pitch in to prepare meals. Kids are more apt to eat healthful foods when they have a role in preparation, too. It's a fun activity. And it'll provide more time to be together as a family—during meal preparation and at mealtime. Try to eat together without distractions, including digital devices. This will help you eat more slowly, fully enjoy the meal you've prepared, and stay better connected as a family.

31. **Regroup on the weekend.** Press the reset button by taking a look at the ingredients you have or don't have on hand. Make a list of what you need for the week ahead. And do some pre-prep for Monday through Friday to help yourself steer clear of weekday stress.

32. **Outsource your cooking.** If you have cash to spare, hire a personal chef. Request recipes you'd like him or her to make from *The All-Natural Diabetes Cookbook, 2nd Edition*, too. That's called fuss-free cooking, for sure!

33. **Get schooled.** Cooking classes for the public are popping up everywhere, including in professional culinary schools, in local cookware stores, and in the workplace. Even if you've been cooking for decades, it can make your entire cooking process flow more smoothly and quickly if you know proper culinary techniques, beginning with the ideal way to hold a chef's knife. Then you can "hire" yourself!

THE ALL-NATURAL, DIABETES-FRIENDLY SUBSTITUTION LIST

To make a recipe healthier, ingredient substitutions for cooking or baking are not always necessarily tasty substitutions. For instance, using fat-free mayonnaise instead of regular mayonnaise will significantly decrease calories, but will also decrease flavor satisfaction. And, unfortunately, these changes can add preservatives or other not-so-real ingredients that your body doesn't need.

Below is a sampling of 10 simple yet succulent ingredient swaps to try at home—naturally. They can help you reduce calories or improve the overall nutritional quality of your meals without sacrificing flavor. Most of these swaps (and many more) are already used in the recipes of *The All-Natural Diabetes Cookbook, 2nd Edition*.

Instead Of	Try
1/4 cup sour cream	1/4 cup low-fat or fat-free plain greek yogurt, quark, or petite crème
2 tablespoons mayonnaise (for salads)	1 tablespoon organic or non-GMO mayonnaise + 1 tablespoon low-fat or fat-free plain greek yogurt + pinch of lemon zest or splash of hot pepper sauce
2 tablespoons mayonnaise (on sandwiches)	2 tablespoons hummus, black bean dip, tzatziki, or guacamole
1 tablespoon butter (in sautéing)	2 teaspoons grapeseed oil, extra-virgin olive oil, or other heart-friendly oil
1 tablespoon butter (in baking)	1 1/2 teaspoons grapeseed oil, extra-virgin olive oil, or other heart-friendly oil + 1 teaspoon unsalted butter
1 cup sugar (in baking)	3/4 cup turbinado or coconut palm sugar + pinch of sweet spice, such as ground cinnamon, and/or extra 1/4 teaspoon pure vanilla extract
1 ounce regular cheese	3/4 ounce high-flavored regular cheese, such as extra-sharp instead of mild cheddar cheese
1 cup all-purpose flour (in baking)	1 cup whole-wheat pastry flour
1 teaspoon salt	1/2 teaspoon sea salt + 1/2 teaspoon grated lemon zest + up to twice the amount of herbs or spices already in recipe
1/4 cup bottled salad dressing	1/4 cup cubed fruit blended with 1 tablespoon extra-virgin olive oil + 1 tablespoon vinegar of choice

What's In Season?

When produce is in season, it's at its peak of ripeness, nutritional value, and flavor. It's usually least expensive then, too! While you can find many fruits and vegetables all year long, different produce varieties peak at different times of the year . . . and seasonality and availability will vary in different parts of the country.

Keep in mind, if you're having difficulty finding a certain fresh fruit or vegetable, it may be out of season in your area. When out of season locally, it's often better to purchase frozen, not fresh. Frozen produce is picked and frozen at its peak of ripeness, nutritional value, and flavor.

Ideally, determine first what produce is seasonal, then pick recipes and plan your menu based on what's at peak availability. To help determine which vegetables or fruits are at their seasonal best, visit your local farmers' market or other market that specializes in locally available vegetables, herbs, and fruits. If it's there, it's in season. You can also check out Sustainable Table's Seasonal Food Guide where you'll find seasonality charts for your area: www.sustainabletable.org/seasonalfoodguide/.

16 SIMPLE, SEASONAL, AND SCRUMPTIOUS MENUS

Pick your season...then pick a menu. Many are ideal for special occasions. But don't feel you need to stick to the meal theme. Sit down to a holiday dinner any day. Celebrate Fat Tuesday on a Wednesday. Have a Super Bowl feast while watching the Academy Awards. Each deliciously easy menu includes one serving of a recipe from *The All-Natural Diabetes Cookbook, 2nd Edition.*

Spring

Spring Break Breakfast

Take a vacation from your breakfast routine with this sunny start to your day—even if it's a not-so-sunny day.

- **Blanco Huevos Rancheros** (page 30)
- 1 fresh peach, sliced
- 1/4 cup low-fat cottage or ricotta cheese

Lovely Ladies' Lunch

Men will also enjoy this beautifully balanced meal, not just the ladies.

- **Caramelized Pear, Sage, and Gorgonzola Quesadilla** (page 90)
- 3 ounces roasted chicken breast with 1/8 teaspoon minced fresh rosemary
- 8 roasted asparagus spears, spritzed with extra-virgin olive oil, served with a lemon wedge

Cinco de Mayo Fiesta

Celebrate this spring holiday with a margarita on the rocks, too.

- 2 cups baby spinach salad, dressed with a splash of grapeseed oil and raspberry vinegar
- **Tequila-Lime Chicken and Spinach Fettuccine** (page 236)

Memorial Day Dinner

Add worldly flair to your next meal with a bountiful bowl of interesting flavors, colors, and textures. Don't forget the chopsticks.

- 2 cups baby arugula salad, dressed with a splash of toasted sesame oil and lime juice
- **Sesame-Ginger Bell Pepper and Soba Noodle Bowl** (page 232)
- 2 ounces grilled lean filet mignon, thinly sliced and served on top of the noodle bowl

Beach Bag Lunch

Headed to the beach? You'll be refreshed by this light Mediterranean lunch. No utensils are required.

- **Stuffed Lemony Hummus Pita** (page 218)
- 1 cup english cucumber slices
- 1/2 cup grape tomatoes
- 10 roasted almonds
- 1 fresh plum or fig

Red, White & Blue Cookout

Celebrate your Independence Day with fireworks for your palate.

- 3 ounces spice-rubbed, grilled wild salmon
- 3 vegetable skewers—each secured with 3 cherry tomatoes, 3 white onion wedges, and 4 boiled baby blue potato halves—each brushed with 1/2 teaspoon extra-virgin olive oil and grilled
- **Balsamic Strawberries** (page 314)

It's Too Hot to Cook

Who needs soup and salad—or sandwich and salad? How about salad and salad? Better yet, try this trio of salads!

- **Bow Tie Macaroni Salad** (page 140)
- 2 cups mesclun salad, dressed with a splash of extra-virgin olive oil and aged balsamic vinegar
- 1 cup mixed berry fruit salad

Right-Sized Bikini and Swim Trunk Meal

Need to squeeze into that bathing suit? Just dive into these light yet luscious bites and you won't need to fret about its itsy-bitsy-ness.

- 1/2 cup shelled organic edamame with sea salt to taste
- **Fresh Tarragon Chicken Salad on Rye** (page 204)
- 15 red seedless grapes

Autumn

Fall Fruit Harvest Breakfast

Savor a fresh fall fruit in each bite. Kids will even give this brightly flavored meal an "A" as their back-to-school breakfast favorite.

- **Granny Smith Breakfast Sausage Patties** (page 42)
- 1 piece whole-grain toast with 1 tablespoon mashed banana
- 1/2 cup fat-free plain yogurt stirred with 3 tablespoons mashed banana and 1/2 cup blueberries

Spooky Halloween Supper

Here's a scary yet lip-smacking dinner for this trick-filled holiday.

- **Simple Gazpacho** (call it "Chilled Blood Sipper"; page 172)
- 1 boiled egg, halved, lightly drizzled with 2 teaspoons ketchup (call it "Screaming Eyeballs")
- 1 cup low-fat vegetarian chili, served with a cinnamon stick (call it "Witch's Goulash")
- 5 large black olives (for your fingertips!)

Election Night Nibbles

Go vote! Then plan a no-cook dinner that's ideal for grazing throughout the exciting (or frustrating) election night news coverage.

- 6 cooked, chilled, large shrimp with 2 tablespoons cocktail sauce
- 1 cup raw veggie strips, such as jicama and mixed bell peppers, with 2 tablespoons tzatziki or other yogurt dip
- 1 small apple, sliced, with 2 tablespoons natural, no-salt-added peanut butter
- **Pomegranate Martini** (to toast the winners—or losers; page 310)

Thanksgiving Dinner Anytime

Thanksgiving is such a delicious day. Enjoy its flavors any time you wish, with family or friends you're thankful to have.

- **Creamy Chestnut Soup** (page 184)
- 3 ounces natural, roasted, sliced turkey breast with 2 teaspoons whole-berry cranberry sauce
- 1/2 cup mashed pumpkin or sweet potato with 1/2 teaspoon butter
- 1 cup steamed green beans with 1 tablespoon pan-toasted, natural sliced almonds

Hometown Holiday Dinner

Lean meat or poultry doesn't need to be doused in gravy. It's mouthwatering when served on this memorable bean "bed." Best of all, this holiday meal includes a perfectly portioned slice of pie.

- 3 ounces roasted or broiled lean grass-fed lamb chop or poultry breast, seasoned as desired
- **Stewed Rosemary Bean Bed** (page 276)
- 1 cup roasted, sliced beets, dressed with 1 teaspoon aged balsamic vinegar
- 1 thin slice pumpkin pie

Savory Super Bowl Party Buffet

You can root for all the players on this party platter. It's a touchdown for your taste buds.

- **Minted Middle Eastern Meatballs** (page 112)
- 1/2 whole-grain pita
- 1 cup raw broccoli florets or other veggies with 3 tablespoons hummus or tzatziki
- 1/2 ounce organic blue corn tortilla chips with 2 tablespoons salsa or hummus

Not-So-Fat Tuesday Plate

You'll get jazzed up about this New Orleans–inspired meal.

- 1 (1 1/2-ounce) slice natural, lean, low-sodium (uncured) baked ham, oven-heated or pan-grilled, sprinkled with 1 tablespoon chopped pecans and 1 teaspoon pure maple syrup
- **Cajun Grains** (page 266)
- 1 cup steamed swiss chard, kale, or spinach, with an orange or lemon wedge

Valentine's Dinner for Couples (or Singles)

Ladies, this will be a pleasing meal for your partner. Guys, same goes for you!

- 2 cups baby spinach salad with 1/2 cup frozen artichoke hearts (thawed) and 1/2 tablespoon pan-toasted pine nuts, dressed with a splash of red wine vinegar and extra-virgin olive oil
- **Steak with Red Wine Reduction Sauce** (page 240)
- 1 cup wild mushrooms, sautéed with 1 teaspoon extra-virgin olive oil, sprinkled with fresh herbs of choice
- 6 steamed baby carrots, sprinkled with fresh herbs of choice
- 1/2 cup cooked quinoa or whole-wheat couscous with 1/2 tablespoon pan-toasted pine nuts, sprinkled with fresh herbs of choice

The
Natural
Recipe
Collection

Breakfasts

Buckwheat Banana Pancakes with Walnuts

These hearty pancakes contain buckwheat flour. You might be surprised to know that buckwheat is not wheat at all; it's an herb of Russian descent. Though the end result here is 100% all-American goodness.

1/4 cup buckwheat flour

3 tablespoons whole-wheat pastry flour

1 teaspoon double-acting baking powder

1/2 teaspoon sea salt

2 teaspoons cold, unsalted butter, cut into pieces

1 1/2 teaspoons honey or pure maple syrup

1 large egg

1/2 cup unsweetened vanilla almond or other plant-based milk

2 large fully ripened bananas, peeled

2 tablespoons chopped walnuts

Serves: 4 | Serving Size: 2 pancakes
Prep Time: 16 minutes | Cooking Time: 16 minutes

DIRECTIONS

1. In a medium bowl, combine the flours, baking powder, salt, butter, and honey into a finely crumbled mixture with a pastry blender or potato masher.

2. In a large bowl, whisk together the egg and almond milk. Add the flour mixture to the egg mixture and whisk until well combined. Let stand for 5 minutes. Mash one banana and set aside; very thinly slice the other banana and stir the slices into the batter.

3. Lightly coat a large, flat skillet or griddle with cooking spray (see Fresh Fact) and place over medium heat. Spoon about 1/4 cup batter per pancake on the hot skillet. Cook pancakes in batches until lightly browned, about 2 minutes per side. Keep cooked pancakes warm on a plate loosely covered with foil.

4. Top pancakes with mashed banana and walnuts, and serve.

Choices/Exchanges: 1/2 starch, 1 fruit, 1/2 lean protein, 1 fat
Per Serving: calories 170, calories from fat 60, total fat 7g, saturated fat 2g, trans fat 0g, cholesterol 50mg, sodium 450mg, potassium 365mg, total carbohydrate 26g, dietary fiber 4g, sugars 9g, protein 5g, phosphorus 125mg

FRESH FACT

Kick the can. Make your own cooking spray with your favorite oil. Try grapeseed oil, extra-virgin olive oil, peanut oil, or another heart-friendly favorite. If you prefer one oil for all cooking purposes, choose grapeseed; its mild flavor will work well with any recipe and it can withstand high heat. Just purchase a pump-spray bottle designed for kitchen use, fill, and spritz—naturally.

FAST FIX

Create your own pancake mix. Stir together the flours, baking powder, and salt, and store in a sealed jar or other food container. Label and date your mix—it'll keep for weeks!

Savory Asparagus Oatmeal

I have to admit, I was never a fan of oatmeal growing up. I was a cold cereal kind of kid. I learned to appreciate hot cereal as an adult. But it wasn't until I started making it in a savory way—with vegetables and herbs—that I became a true aficionada of oatmeal. My taste buds adore it. I actually enjoy the cold leftovers, too. I hope you become as much of a fan of this asparagus oatmeal as I am.

4 cups cold water

1 pound asparagus spears, trimmed, cut into 5 pieces each on the diagonal, divided

2 teaspoons fresh lemon juice

3/4 teaspoon sea salt

1/2 teaspoon freshly ground black pepper

2 cups old-fashioned oats

2 scallions, green and white part, minced

1 tablespoon finely chopped fresh dill

2 teaspoons extra-virgin olive oil

DIRECTIONS

1. Bring the water, all of the asparagus except the tips, lemon juice, salt, and pepper to a boil in a large saucepan.

2. Stir in the oats, asparagus tips, and scallions and reduce heat to medium. Cook, while stirring, until the oats and asparagus are fully cooked, about 6 minutes. Remove from heat and stir in the dill and olive oil.

3. Transfer the oatmeal to individual bowls and serve.

Choices/Exchanges: 2 starch, 1 vegetable, 1/2 fat
Per Serving: calories 190, calories from fat 45, total fat 5g, saturated fat 1g, trans fat 0g, cholesterol 0mg, sodium 450mg, potassium 155mg, total carbohydrate 30g, dietary fiber 5g, sugars 2g, protein 7g, phosphorus 35mg

FRESH FACT

Be buddies with breakfast. Eating healthful portions regularly can build stable eating patterns. While it may seem counterintuitive, regular breakfast eaters are actually more likely to have a healthy weight than breakfast skippers.

FOOD FLAIR

This savory oatmeal recipe is versatile. Prepare it with various herbs. Or mix and match different vegetables and fresh herbs in this oatmeal. Try these combinations: grape tomatoes and basil, diced bell peppers and oregano, sliced zucchini and tarragon, or baby spinach and dill. And for a heartier meal, top each bowl with a poached egg.

Blanco Huevos Rancheros

Though egg yolks are filled with good nutrition, using all egg whites here helps me include other delicious, nutritious, yet rich ingredients, such as avocado and cheese. It's a Mexican-inspired recipe keeper for breakfast or brunch—or beyond.

4 (6-inch) organic corn tortillas

Natural oil cooking spray

8 large egg whites OR 1 cup 100% pasteurized liquid egg whites

1/4 teaspoon freshly ground black pepper

1/8 teaspoon sea salt

3 tablespoons shredded pepper jack or monterey jack cheese

1/2 Hass avocado, peeled, pitted, and diced

1/4 cup tomatillo (green) salsa or Salsa Verde (page 76)

1/4 cup fat-free plain greek yogurt or quark

1 small jalapeño pepper, seeded and minced

1 tablespoon chopped fresh cilantro

Serves: 2 | Serving Size: 2 topped tortillas
Prep Time: 15 minutes | Cooking Time: 13 minutes

DIRECTIONS

1. Preheat the oven to 475°F. Lightly coat both sides of the corn tortillas with cooking spray and place on a baking sheet. Bake until crisp and lightly browned, about 4 minutes per side. Remove from the oven and let cool on the baking sheet.

2. Meanwhile, place a large nonstick skillet over medium heat. Add the egg whites and scramble until done, about 5 minutes. Immediately stir in the pepper, salt, and cheese.

3. Place a scoop of cheesy egg whites on top of each crisp tortilla. Top each with equal portions of the avocado, salsa, yogurt, jalapeño, and cilantro, and serve.

Choices/Exchanges: 1 1/2 starch, 2 1/2 medium-fat protein
Per Serving: calories 310, calories from fat 100, total fat 11g, saturated fat 3g, trans fat 0g, cholesterol 10mg, sodium 690mg, potassium 610mg, total carbohydrate 29g, dietary fiber 6g, sugars 5g, protein 23g, phosphorus 275mg

FOOD FLAIR

Use the jalapeño seeds in this dish if you like an extra "kick" in the morning. And if you want still more eye-opening zip, squirt each serving of this dish with a lime wedge.

MORE THAN FOUR?

This recipe is an impressive morning meal for company. It can easily be doubled, tripled, or quadrupled. Just use an extra-large pan for scrambling the egg whites. Also, have all the other ingredients prepped and lined up buffet-style to top the tortillas once the egg whites are scrambled and hot. Toss the avocado with the tomatillo salsa; it'll help prevent the avocado from browning as it stands.

Heirloom Caprese Omelet

Enjoy a little taste of Italy right in your own home. It'll be a transporting experience when you make this omelet with any variety of heirloom tomatoes picked up fresh at your local farmers' market. But if you can't find heirloom, go for vine-ripened tomatoes, which are usually at their peak in late summer.

10 large egg whites OR 1 1/4 cups 100% pasteurized liquid egg whites

2 large eggs

1 tablespoon cold water

1/2 teaspoon sea salt

1/4 teaspoon freshly ground black pepper

2 teaspoons extra-virgin olive oil, divided

1 large clove garlic, minced, divided

1/3 cup shredded part-skim mozzarella cheese, divided

1 large heirloom or vine-ripened tomato, cut crosswise into 12 thin slices

12 large fresh basil leaves

1 1/2 teaspoons aged balsamic or white balsamic vinegar

DIRECTIONS

1. In a medium bowl, whisk together the egg whites, eggs, water, salt, and pepper until well combined.

2. Heat 1 teaspoon of the oil in a large nonstick skillet over medium heat. Add half of the garlic and sauté until fragrant, about 1 minute. Pour in half the egg mixture. Using a spatula, lift the edges of the eggs as they cook, letting the uncooked part run underneath until the omelet is set and the bottom is lightly browned, about 4 minutes. Sprinkle with half the cheese. Slide out onto a platter, folding omelet over. Slice in half and cover with foil to keep warm.

3. Repeat the process with the remaining oil, garlic, egg mixture, and cheese.

4. Top each omelet half with 3 tomato slices and 3 basil leaves. Drizzle with the vinegar and serve.

Choices/Exchanges: 2 lean protein, 1 fat
Per Serving: calories 140, calories from fat 60, total fat 7g, saturated fat 2g, trans fat 0g, cholesterol 100mg, sodium 530mg, potassium 295mg, total carbohydrate 4g, dietary fiber 1g, sugars 2g, protein 15g, phosphorus 125mg

FRESH FACT

Once you bring tomatoes home from the farmers' market or grocery store, keep them on the counter, not in the refrigerator. Refrigerating unripe tomatoes halts the ripening process and adversely affects their texture and flavor.

Sausage-Spinach Scramble with Caramelized Onions

The balance of flavors in this breakfast dish will have you scrambling for it regularly. And don't worry if the amount of onion seems like a lot. The large amount cooks down to a little. And the onions are exceptionally sweet when caramelized.

1 teaspoon extra-virgin olive oil

1 large Vidalia or other sweet onion, very thinly sliced

1 large clove garlic, minced

8 frozen, precooked, natural chicken or turkey breakfast sausage links, cut crosswise into 1/8-inch slices (5 1/2 ounces total)

6 large egg whites OR 3/4 cup 100% pasteurized liquid egg whites

1 large egg

1/4 teaspoon freshly ground black pepper

1/8 teaspoon sea salt

1 (5-ounce) package fresh baby spinach (5 cups packed)

1 tablespoon freshly grated parmigiano-reggiano cheese

4 lemon wedges (optional)

DIRECTIONS

1. Heat the oil in a large nonstick skillet over medium heat. Add the onion and cook until rich golden brown, stirring occasionally, about 15 minutes. Add the garlic and sausage and sauté until the sausage is heated through, about 3 minutes.

2. Meanwhile, in a medium bowl, whisk together the egg whites, egg, pepper, and salt.

3. Pour the eggs over the caramelized onion–sausage mixture in the skillet and scramble until done, about 3 minutes. Remove from heat.

4. Stir in the spinach until just wilted. (If the pan is not big enough to hold the spinach, combine everything in a large bowl, then quickly reheat in the skillet.) Sprinkle with the cheese. Serve immediately with the lemon wedges, if using.

Choices/Exchanges: 1 1/2 vegetable, 2 medium-fat protein
Per Serving: calories 190, calories from fat 90, total fat 10g, saturated fat 2.5g, trans fat 0g, cholesterol 110mg, sodium 470mg, potassium 465mg, total carbohydrate 9g, dietary fiber 2g, sugars 5g, protein 15g, phosphorus 140mg

FRESH FACT

Spinach and egg yolk—two ingredients in this morning meal—both contain the antioxidants lutein and zeaxanthin. These antioxidants may help protect against age-related macular degeneration, a cause of irreversible blindness. Other dark leafy greens, such as swiss chard and kale, contain these nutrients, too. So feel free to play with other greens here.

FOOD FLAIR

Got vegetarians at the table? This entrée can be made with vegetarian breakfast links or patties, too. Read the ingredient lists on packages and choose the "cleanest" product, one that's free of hydrolyzed vegetable protein and artificial flavors.

Herbed Eggs and Ham

Go ahead…have some fun with your food—then present your plate with pride! It doesn't get much more fun than eating cartoon-like green food. This Dr. Seuss–inspired dish is not only a kid-pleaser, it's an entire family–pleaser.

2 (2-ounce-thick) slices natural, lean, uncured baked or smoked ham, each cut in half

1 large clove garlic

1/2 cup loosely packed fresh basil leaves

1/4 cup loosely packed fresh flat-leaf parsley leaves

6 large egg whites OR 3/4 cup 100% pasteurized liquid egg whites

3 large eggs

2 teaspoons extra-virgin olive oil

2 teaspoons fresh lemon juice

Pinch sea salt (1/16 teaspoon)

1 teaspoon unsalted butter

Serves: 4 | Serving Size: Rounded 1/2 cup eggs plus 1/2 ounce ham
Prep Time: 12 minutes | Cooking Time: 20 minutes

DIRECTIONS

1. Preheat the oven to 275°F. Wrap the ham in foil and warm in the oven up to 15 minutes.

2. Meanwhile, purée the garlic, basil, parsley, egg whites, eggs, oil, lemon juice, and salt in a blender on low speed until the egg mixture is an even, light-green color, about 1 minute.

3. Melt the butter in a nonstick skillet over medium heat. Add the egg mixture and scramble until the eggs are done, about 3 minutes.

4. Serve the eggs with a warm ham slice. Garnish with fresh basil or parsley sprigs, if desired.

Choices/Exchanges: 2 1/2 lean protein, 1 fat
Per Serving: calories 150, calories from fat 80, total fat 9g, saturated fat 2.5g, trans fat 0g, cholesterol 155mg, sodium 520mg, potassium 255mg, total carbohydrate 2g, dietary fiber 0g, sugars 1g, protein 16g, phosphorus 145mg

FAST FIX

Blend the green egg mixture the night before you need it. Store it in a covered container and refrigerate. Shake the container before scrambling. You can also quickly warm the ham in the microwave or pan-grill it instead of heating the ham in the oven.

Eggs Benedict with Silken Hollandaise Sauce

There are some rich foods that aren't easily made over into flavorful, healthful choices. Thankfully, Eggs Benedict is a dish that's done here successfully—and succulently. The silken tofu gives the sauce a velvety mouth feel that's unmatched. Plus, the sauce is so peppy you may never go back to regular hollandaise sauce.

4 ounces organic silken tofu, undrained (1/2 cup)

Juice of 1 small lemon (2 tablespoons)

2 tablespoons fat-free evaporated milk

1 teaspoon unsalted butter

2 teaspoons dijon mustard

1 teaspoon worcestershire sauce

Pinch ground cayenne pepper

3 whole-grain english muffins, split and toasted

6 (3/4-ounce) slices natural, lean, uncured baked or smoked ham, pan-grilled or oven-heated

6 medium eggs, poached (see Fresh Fact)

Serves: 6 | Serving Size: 1 topped muffin half
Prep Time: 20 minutes | Cooking Time: 10 minutes (including egg poaching time)

DIRECTIONS

1. Purée the tofu, lemon juice, evaporated milk, butter, mustard, worcester-shire sauce, and cayenne pepper in a blender on low speed until smooth, about 30 seconds.

2. Place the mixture in a small saucepan over medium-low heat. Simmer until hot, about 5 minutes.

3. Meanwhile, top each toasted muffin half with a ham slice, then a poached egg. Top each with about 3 tablespoons of the hot silken hollandaise sauce and serve.

Choices/Exchanges: 1 starch, 1 1/2 medium-fat protein
Per Serving: calories 190, calories from fat 60, total fat 7g, saturated fat 2.5g, trans fat 0g, cholesterol 175mg, sodium 530mg, potassium 255mg, total carbohydrate 17g, dietary fiber 2g, sugars 4g, protein 14g, phosphorus 235mg

FRESH FACT

To poach eggs, bring about 3 inches of water to boil in a large (12-inch) shallow skillet over high heat. Turn off the heat and add eggs at once by breaking them directly into the water. Immediately cover pan with a tight-fitting lid. Allow eggs to cook undisturbed until done as desired, about 4 minutes. Remove the eggs with a perforated spatula or large slotted spoon and drain on plain unbleached paper towels.

FOOD FLAIR

For a change of taste, enjoy with steamed, seasoned spinach, kale, or roasted asparagus in place of the ham. Sprinkle with cayenne pepper for extra pep.

Mexican Baked Egg Whites in Tomato Cups

Enjoying the natural flavors of good nutrition is easy with these clever "cups." This eye-opening entrée, where the cups are actually tomatoes, will impress a significant other—and you. You can use smaller or larger tomatoes for the cups, too; adjust the amount of egg whites accordingly. Each tomato cup should be about 3/4 full of egg white before you add the salsa. Then serve with warm organic corn tortillas and fresh seasonal fruit for a fully satisfying breakfast for two.

4 medium, firm, vine-ripened tomatoes

Pinch sea salt (1/16 teaspoon)

4 large egg whites OR 1/2 cup 100% pasteurized liquid egg whites

1/4 cup salsa of choice

1/2 Hass avocado, peeled, pitted, and cut crosswise into 12 slices

Juice of 1/2 lime (1 tablespoon)

2 tablespoons chopped fresh cilantro

Serves: 2 | Serving Size: 2 tomato cups
Prep Time: 12 minutes | Cooking Time: 25 minutes

DIRECTIONS

1. Preheat the oven to 450°F. Slice about 3/4 inch off the top of each tomato. With a spoon or grapefruit spoon, scoop out the insides of each tomato to form tomato cups; reserve insides for another use.

2. Place tomato cups on an unbleached parchment paper–lined baking pan, or place each into a ramekin or small, round baking dish. Sprinkle with the salt. Add 1 egg white to each tomato cup and top each with 1 tablespoon salsa.

3. Bake until the egg whites are firm, about 25 minutes. Remove from the oven and top each cup with 3 avocado slices arranged like a fan. Drizzle with lime juice, top with cilantro, and serve.

Choices/Exchanges: 2 vegetable, 1 lean protein, 1 fat
Per Serving: calories 150, calories from fat 50, total fat 6g, saturated fat 1g, trans fat 0g, cholesterol 0mg, sodium 420mg, potassium 970mg, total carbohydrate 16g, dietary fiber 6g, sugars 8g, protein 11g, phosphorus 100mg

FRESH FACT

If you have an avocado that's not quite fully ripened, place it in a paper bag at least overnight. It will be more luscious when ripe. If you want the avocado flavor to pop without reaching for the salt shaker, a squirt of lime juice can do the trick.

FOOD FLAIR

There's no need for food waste. Finely dice the reserved tomato tops and use as a garnish. Add the scooped-out tomato pulp to a soup, stew, or the simmering liquid of brown rice. Also, freeze the unused egg yolks for use in other recipes; just whisk 4 yolks with 1/8 teaspoon sea salt before freezing.

Granny Smith Breakfast Sausage Patties

Sausage as a main dish? Sure. These substantial and scrumptious patties are best served two at a time for a morning entrée. They can be served singly as a side dish, too. The wholesome apples and oats make these burger-like patties well balanced and deliciously moist.

8 ounces ground chicken breast

4 ounces grass-fed lean ground beef sirloin or ground turkey (about 93% lean)

1 medium Granny Smith apple, cored, peeled, and coarsely grated

2/3 cup plain quick-cooking, whole-grain oats

1/4 cup coarsely grated red onion

1/4 cup chopped fresh flat-leaf parsley

1 tablespoon finely chopped fresh sage

1 teaspoon minced fresh rosemary (optional)

3/4 teaspoon sea salt

1/2 teaspoon freshly ground black pepper

1 large egg, lightly beaten

DIRECTIONS

1. In a large bowl, combine by hand all ingredients. Form the mixture into 8 patties (use about 1/3 cup mixture for each patty).

2. Place a large nonstick skillet over medium heat. Cook the patties in batches until well done, about 4 minutes per side, flipping only once. Remove the cooked patties to a plate and keep covered with foil until all the patties are done. Serve warm.

Choices/Exchanges: 1 starch, 2 1/2 lean protein
Per Serving: calories 190, calories from fat 45, total fat 5g, saturated fat 1.5g, trans fat 0g, cholesterol 95mg, sodium 500mg, potassium 325mg, total carbohydrate 17g, dietary fiber 3g, sugars 6g, protein 21g, phosphorus 225mg

FAST FIX

You can form the patties in the evening, cover and refrigerate them, then cook in the morning. Cook the chilled patties until well done, about 5 minutes per side.

MORE THAN FOUR?

Prepare 16 mini patties with this recipe. Cook until well done, about 3–4 minutes per side. Serve two to each person as a side dish for breakfast or brunch.

Summer Veggie Hash Browns

You'll fall for this colorful summertime side that takes advantage of farmers' market finds. Yellow summer squash, zucchini, and peppers are on full taste display here instead of typical potatoes. While this hash brown recipe provides a delightful way to enjoy veggies in your morning meal, do savor this side dish anytime.

1 1/2 tablespoons extra-virgin olive oil

2 large shallots, diced

1 medium (8-ounce) yellow summer squash, cubed

1 medium (8-ounce) zucchini, cubed

1 medium red, orange, or green bell pepper, diced

1 small jalapeño pepper, with some seeds, minced

1 1/2 teaspoons apple cider vinegar

1 large clove garlic, minced

1 1/2 teaspoons minced fresh rosemary

3/4 teaspoon sea salt

Serves: 4 | Serving Size: 3/4 cup
Prep Time: 15 minutes | Cooking Time: 18 minutes

DIRECTIONS

1. Heat the oil in a large nonstick skillet over medium heat. Add the shallots, yellow squash, zucchini, bell pepper, and jalapeño and stir to combine. Cover and let cook until the yellow squash and zucchini are just softened, about 8 minutes, stirring once.

2. Add the vinegar, garlic, rosemary, and salt. Increase heat to medium high, sauté until the vegetables are lightly caramelized, about 8 minutes, and serve.

Choices/Exchanges: 2 vegetable, 1 fat
Per Serving: calories 90, calories from fat 50, total fat 6g, saturated fat 1g, trans fat 0g, cholesterol 0mg, sodium 450mg, potassium 425mg, total carbohydrate 9g, dietary fiber 2g, sugars 5g, protein 2g, phosphorus 65mg

FOOD FLAIR

This versatile recipe makes a lovely omelet filling for breakfast or pasta topping for dinner. Or chill hash brown leftovers and serve in a turkey or cheese sandwich to boost your veggie quotient at lunchtime.

Portobello Bacon Strips

This recipe proves that bodacious vegan bacon can be a reality. These portobello strips become mini sized as the natural water of the fresh mushrooms evaporates during roasting. That's what makes these strips so crispy. They're so tasty, too. These portobello bacon pieces actually do have the smoky flavor essence of real bacon. But they're way better for you since they're made from vegetables after all.

1 1/2 teaspoons turbinado or coconut palm sugar

1/2 teaspoon sea salt

1/4 teaspoon plus 1/8 teaspoon smoked paprika

1/4 teaspoon chili powder

1/4 teaspoon garlic powder

2 jumbo (about 6-inch diameter) portobello mushroom caps, thinly sliced (1/8 inch thick)

2 tablespoons extra-virgin olive oil

Serves: 3 | Serving Size: About 10 pieces
Prep Time: 10 minutes | Cooking Time: 2 hours

DIRECTIONS

1. Preheat the oven to 275°F. In a small bowl, stir together the sugar, salt, paprika, chili powder, and garlic powder.

2. Add the mushrooms to a medium bowl, drizzle with the oil, and gently toss to fully coat. Sprinkle with the seasoning mixture and gently toss to fully coat. Arrange in a single layer on two large, unbleached parchment paper–lined baking sheets.

3. Roast until reduced in size by about two-thirds and deeply caramelized, about 1 hour and 15 minutes. There's no need to stir or flip over during roasting. Turn off the oven and let strips continue to crisp in the warm oven for 45 minutes.

4. Remove from the oven and cool on the pan on a rack to allow to further crisp, at least 15 minutes, then serve. If desired, prepare and store strips in the refrigerator overnight; bring to room temperature before serving.

Choices/Exchanges: 1 vegetable, 2 fat
Per Serving: calories 110, calories from fat 80, total fat 9g, saturated fat 1.5g, trans fat 0g, cholesterol 0mg, sodium 400mg, potassium 360mg, total carbohydrate 8g, dietary fiber 1g, sugars 5g, protein 2g, phosphorus 105mg

FRESH FACT

One unique plant nutrient in mushrooms is called ergosterol. When exposed to the sun, it naturally converts to vitamin D—the "sunshine" vitamin. So if you want to be friendly to your bones, eat more mushrooms. Plus, preliminary research suggests that having higher vitamin-D levels may play a beneficial role in the health of those with or at risk for diabetes.

Homestyle Banana Bread Bites

When I was growing up, my mother often baked banana bread, froze it, and sliced it into paper-thin slices for my after-school snack. I thought it was such a treat when semi-frozen—like having dessert before dinner. Here, I've updated her recipe. It's now perfect for a little breakfast bite… just grab a square along with a café au lait and go!

2 tablespoons grapeseed or safflower oil

2 tablespoons unsalted butter, melted

2/3 cup turbinado or coconut palm sugar

3 large egg whites OR 6 tablespoons 100% pasteurized liquid egg whites

3 large extra-ripe bananas, mashed (about 1 1/3 cups)

1 1/2 teaspoons pure vanilla extract

1 1/2 cups whole-wheat pastry flour

1 teaspoon baking soda

1/4 teaspoon sea salt

1/4 cup chopped walnuts

Serves: 16 | Serving Size: 1 square
Prep Time: 20 minutes | Cooking Time: 30–35 minutes

DIRECTIONS

1. Preheat the oven to 350°F. Lightly coat an 8 × 8-inch nonstick baking pan with cooking spray.

2. In a large mixing bowl, whisk together the oil, melted butter, and sugar. Add the egg whites and whisk until well combined. Add the mashed bananas and vanilla extract and whisk until well combined.

3. In a medium bowl, sift or whisk together the flour, baking soda, and salt. Add to the banana mixture and stir until just combined. Pour the batter into the pan. Sprinkle the walnuts on top and then very lightly press them onto the batter.

4. Bake until springy to the touch, about 30–35 minutes. Cool on a rack, then slice into squares. Serve warm, at room temperature, or chilled.

Choices/Exchanges: 1/2 starch, 1 carbohydrate, 1 fat
Per Serving: calories 140, calories from fat 40, total fat 4.5g, saturated fat 1.5g, trans fat 0g, cholesterol 5mg, sodium 125mg, potassium 155mg, total carbohydrate 24g, dietary fiber 2g, sugars 12g, protein 2g, phosphorus 50mg

FRESH FACT

Instead of refined sugar, try turbinado or coconut palm sugar. Turbinado sugar is a slightly coarser, more natural alternative to its white counterpart. Turbinado is made from the first pressing of the sugar cane, which leaves it with a light, crystal-like brown color and a wonderful flavor from its natural molasses. Coconut palm sugar is basically an all-natural or unrefined brown sugar that's harvested from the nectar of a coconut tree. The bonus: it may help stabilize your blood glucose. In cooking and baking, use the same amount of turbinado or coconut palm sugar for granulated white sugar in a recipe—1 cup for 1 cup.

Blue Ribbon Blueberry Muffins

No need to hunt for a muffin recipe that'll easily fit into your healthful eating plan. This is it. These moist, hearty, and sweet blueberry-loaded muffins are just the right size, too. They're definitely blue ribbon worthy.

1 cup plain unsweetened almond or coconut milk beverage,
    at room temperature

2 tablespoons unrefined (virgin) coconut oil, gently warmed,
    or melted unsalted butter

1 large egg

1/2 teaspoon lemon zest

1/2 teaspoon pure vanilla extract

1/2 teaspoon pure almond extract

3/4 cup turbinado or coconut palm sugar

1 2/3 cups whole-wheat pastry flour

1 1/2 teaspoons double-acting baking powder

3/4 teaspoon sea salt

1 pint fresh blueberries (about 2 cups)

DIRECTIONS

1. Preheat the oven to 375°F. Spray 12 cups of a nonstick muffin tin with cooking spray.

2. In a large bowl, vigorously whisk together the almond milk and coconut oil until combined. Whisk in the egg, lemon zest, and extracts until combined, then whisk in the sugar. In a medium bowl, whisk together the flour, baking powder, and salt. Stir the flour mixture into the almond milk mixture until just combined. Fold in the blueberries.

3. Divide the batter among 12 muffin cups, about 1/3 cup batter per muffin cup. Bake 20 minutes or until firm and springy to the touch. Cool in the pan on a rack. After at least 20 minutes, run a small, flexible spatula or butter knife around the muffin edges and gently remove. Serve at room temperature, chilled, or semi-frozen.

Choices/Exchanges: 1 starch, 1 carbohydrate, 1/2 fat
Per Serving: calories 160, calories from fat 30, total fat 3.5g, saturated fat 2g, trans fat 0g, cholesterol 15mg, sodium 230mg, potassium 110mg, total carbohydrate 30g, dietary fiber 3g, sugars 16g, protein 2g, phosphorus 80mg

FRESH FACT

Local blueberries are in season in the spring and summer. These muffins will taste best then, too. However, if you bake these in the fall or winter, simply use thawed frozen blueberries in the batter instead of fresh.

FAST FIX

Bake and freeze these marvelous morsels. Just place a frozen muffin into a covered container at room temperature overnight and it'll be ready to eat in the morning. Or take a muffin out of the freezer in the morning and enjoy it semi-frozen or chilled. When you eat the muffin semi-frozen, the blueberries inside taste like little mini blueberry popsicles!

PB&J Greek Yogurt Sundae

PB&J lovers, this one's for you! The recipe is in the form of a good-for-you, no-cook breakfast, though it actually looks and tastes like dessert. It's rich in both protein and heart-friendly fats, so it'll carry you well until lunchtime. The sundae is the perfect size for just you. Simply multiply the recipe as needed to make it family friendly.

1 cup fat-free plain greek yogurt, divided

1/4 teaspoon pure vanilla extract

1/2 cup thinly sliced red seedless grapes

2 tablespoons salted roasted peanuts

1 tablespoon 100% concord grape fruit spread

2 teaspoons creamy natural peanut butter

DIRECTIONS

1. In a small bowl, stir together the yogurt and vanilla extract.

2. Arrange 1/3 cup of the yogurt mixture, the grapes, peanuts, and the remaining 2/3 cup yogurt mixture in a large sundae glass or bowl.

3. Dollop with the fruit spread and peanut butter, and serve.

Choices/Exchanges: 1 fruit, 1 fat-free milk, 1/2 other carbohydrate, 3 medium-fat protein
Per Serving: calories 400, calories from fat 140, total fat 15g, saturated fat 2.5g, trans fat 0g, cholesterol 10mg, sodium 260mg, potassium 650mg, total carbohydrate 38g, dietary fiber 3g, sugars 29g, protein 30g, phosphorus 420mg

FOOD FLAIR

There's no need to always stick with the tried and true combination of peanut butter and grape. Shake up tradition and try this breakfast sundae with almond butter and other fruits, like fresh strawberries or peaches, as well as strawberry or peach fruit spread.

Homemade Granola-Raspberry Parfaits

Vegetarians (and nonvegetarians) rejoice! Fiber never tasted so good. This refreshing parfait makes a picture-perfect meal!

1 1/2 cups old-fashioned oats

1/3 cup slivered almonds

3 tablespoons raw wheat germ

2 tablespoons unsalted, shelled sunflower seeds or pepitas

2 teaspoons ground cinnamon

2 tablespoons natural unsweetened apple butter

1 1/2 tablespoons honey or coconut nectar

1 1/3 cups fat-free plain greek yogurt

1 1/3 cups fresh raspberries

Serves: 4 | Serving Size: 1 parfait
Prep Time: 15 minutes | Cooking Time: 25 minutes

DIRECTIONS

1. Preheat the oven to 325°F. In a medium bowl, stir together the oats, almonds, wheat germ, sunflower seeds, and cinnamon.

2. In a small bowl, stir together the apple butter and honey. Add to the oat mixture and stir until thoroughly combined.

3. Spread the mixture evenly in a large baking pan. Bake until toasted and nearly crisp, about 25 minutes, stirring occasionally. Remove from the oven and let cool slightly to further crisp.

4. Layer the granola, yogurt, and raspberries into four parfait, wine, or other beverage glasses, and serve.

Choices/Exchanges: 1 1/2 starch, 1/2 fat-free milk, 1/2 carbohydrate, 1/2 lean protein, 2 fat
Per Serving: calories 320, calories from fat 90, total fat 10g, saturated fat 1g, trans fat 0g, cholesterol 5mg, sodium 30mg, potassium 350mg, total carbohydrate 45g, dietary fiber 9g, sugars 15g, protein 17g, phosphorus 275mg

FRESH FACT

Whole oats are whole grains that contain soluble (or viscous) fiber, which can help reduce blood cholesterol levels. And, in large quantities, soluble fiber may improve blood glucose control. That doesn't mean you can eat "supersized" parfaits! But it does mean it's a good idea to routinely include oats and oatmeal in your eating plan.

FAST FIX

You can prepare this granola ahead of time and store it in an airtight container at room temperature for several days. Instead of taking the time to layer as a parfait, you can simply dollop all the ingredients into a bowl.

Dips, Salsas, and Sauces

Caribbean Black Bean Dip

Break out of a hummus routine by going Caribbean with this quick dip. In this sublime recipe, the combination of beans and avocado creates a velvety texture. Using canned beans is time saving. Go with the organic varieties if you can; they'll be the best tasting and best for the earth. You'll find this bean dip is fully satisfying and extra nutrient-rich when served with bell pepper strips.

1 (15-ounce) can black beans, drained

1/2 Hass avocado, peeled, pitted, and sliced

Juice of 1 lemon (3 tablespoons)

2 tablespoons roughly chopped fresh cilantro

1/4 teaspoon ground cayenne pepper

1/4 teaspoon ground cumin

1/8 teaspoon sea salt

1 scallion, green and white parts, thinly sliced

Serves: 6 | Serving Size: Rounded 1/4 cup
Prep Time: 10 minutes | Cooking Time: 0 minutes

DIRECTIONS

1. Purée all of the ingredients except the scallion in a blender or food processor until smooth.

2. Transfer to a serving bowl, sprinkle with the scallion, and serve.

Choices/Exchanges: 1 starch, 1/2 fat
Per Serving: calories 90, calories from fat 20, total fat 2g, saturated fat 0g, trans fat 0g, cholesterol 0mg, sodium 320mg, potassium 295mg, total carbohydrate 14g, dietary fiber 5g, sugars 0g, protein 5g, phosphorus 85mg

FOOD FLAIR

For best results, refrigerate this creamy dip at least 30 minutes prior to serving. You actually might find it better the next day! For flavor intrigue, stir in 1/8 teaspoon freshly ground nutmeg.

FAST FIX

Create a spice mixture. In a small jar, add 1 tablespoon each of ground cayenne red pepper, ground cumin, and sea salt. Label it "Caribbean Spice Mix." Use 3/4 teaspoon of this mixture whenever you make this dip. Enjoy it as a spice rub for poultry or fish, too.

Jalapeño-Peanut Hummus with Fresh Herbs

I've been a lover of hummus since I was a little child. Creating new versions of it helps bring out the kid in me. Here, I use natural peanut butter instead of the traditional tahini (sesame paste) to create a kicked-up version of this Middle Eastern–style dip. Dunk into it with raw vegetables, such as cucumber slices, or fresh whole-grain pita wedges. Perhaps it'll bring out the kid in you, too.

1 (15-ounce) can chickpeas (garbanzo beans), drained

1 small jalapeño pepper, with or without seeds

1 large clove garlic

1 tablespoon natural creamy peanut butter

Juice of 1 small lemon (2 tablespoons)

1/4 cup cold water or unsweetened green tea

1/4 teaspoon sea salt

3 tablespoons chopped fresh cilantro or flat-leaf parsley

Serves: 6 | Serving Size: 1/4 cup
Prep Time: 10 minutes | Cooking Time: 0 minutes

DIRECTIONS

1. Purée all of the ingredients except the cilantro in a blender or food processor until smooth, adding more water by tablespoonfuls only if necessary.

2. Transfer to a serving bowl, sprinkle with the cilantro, and serve.

Choices/Exchanges: 1/2 starch, 1/2 fat
Per Serving: calories 80, calories from fat 25, total fat 2.5g, saturated fat 0g, trans fat 0g, cholesterol 0mg, sodium 310mg, potassium 135mg, total carbohydrate 11g, dietary fiber 3g, sugars 0g, protein 4g, phosphorus 70mg

FOOD FLAIR

For those who can enjoy healthful fats more liberally, serve this zesty hummus drizzled with extra-virgin olive oil, then topped with fresh flat-leaf parsley. For added crunch, sprinkle with pan-toasted pine nuts. For added color and an aromatic hint of smokiness, add a pinch of smoked paprika.

FRESH FACT

Hummus lovers, your heart will love this news. A meta-analysis of randomized controlled trials published in Canadian Medical Association Journal finds that eating one daily serving (3/4 cup) of chickpeas, beans, lentils, or peas can potentially reduce LDL cholesterol—the "bad" kind of cholesterol—by 5%.

Tex-Mex Layer Dip

Having a casual get-together? This is a fantastically bold dip sure to satisfy everyone at your next big gathering. It's a real party-pleaser. It pairs perfectly with organic, baked blue corn tortilla chips.

1 (15.4- to 16-ounce) can vegetarian refried beans

1/2 teaspoon hot pepper sauce

1 1/2 cups guacamole of choice, such as Classic Guacamole with Tomato (page 70)

3/4 cup fat-free plain greek yogurt or organic low-fat sour cream

Juice of 1 lime (2 tablespoons), divided

3/4 teaspoon chili powder

2 medium vine-ripened tomatoes, seeded and diced

5 scallions, green and white parts, thinly sliced on diagonal

3/4 cup shredded Mexican-style cheese or monterey jack cheese

DIRECTIONS

1. In a small bowl, combine the refried beans and hot pepper sauce. Spread on a large rimmed platter or in a 9 × 13-inch clear glass baking dish. Thinly spread the guacamole on top of the beans.

2. In another bowl, combine the yogurt, 1 tablespoon of the lime juice, and chili powder. Spread the mixture evenly on top of the guacamole layer.

3. Toss the tomatoes with the remaining lime juice in another small bowl. Sprinkle the tomatoes, scallions, and cheese on the yogurt layer, and serve.

Choices/Exchanges: 1/2 starch, 1 fat
Per Serving: calories 70, calories from fat 30, total fat 3.5g, saturated fat 1g, trans fat 0g, cholesterol 5mg, sodium 190mg, potassium 240mg, total carbohydrate 7g, dietary fiber 2g, sugars 1g, protein 4g, phosphorus 85mg

FOOD FLAIR

If you choose to serve this dip warm rather than cool, prepare it without the guacamole layer. Serve the cool guacamole on the side.

FAST FIX

Pick up fresh guacamole from a nearby market. And instead of combining refried beans and hot pepper sauce, shop for spicy canned refried beans or refried beans containing green chilies.

Minted English Cucumber Tzatziki Dip

Traditionally, you might find tzatziki served as a sauce for a Greek gyro. But it's much more versatile than you might realize. Serve it as a dip for veggies or pita chips, a sauce for roasted or grilled poultry, or a condiment for sandwiches or stuffed grape leaves. This tzatziki tastes great for days!

Juice of 1 small lemon (2 tablespoons)

1 1/2 tablespoons extra-virgin olive oil

2 large cloves garlic, minced

1 cup fat-free plain greek yogurt or homemade greek-style yogurt (see Fresh Fact)

1/4 teaspoon sea salt

1/8 teaspoon freshly ground black pepper

1/2 (12-inch) english cucumber with skin, finely diced (1 1/8 cups)

2 tablespoons finely chopped fresh mint

1 tablespoon finely chopped fresh dill

FRESH FACT

To make your own greek-style yogurt, line a mesh strainer with cheesecloth or a double layer of plain unbleached paper towels. Add 18 ounces fat-free plain yogurt into the lined strainer. Place the strainer over a bowl and allow the yogurt to drain, refrigerated, at least 4 hours or overnight. Discard the liquid drained from yogurt (or use the liquid in a smoothie). Makes 1 rounded cup.

DIRECTIONS

1. In a medium bowl, whisk together the lemon juice, olive oil, garlic, yogurt, salt, and pepper. Stir in the cucumber, mint, and dill.

2. Cover, refrigerate until chilled, and serve.

Choices/Exchanges: 1/2 lean protein, 1/2 fat
Per Serving: calories 45, calories from fat 25, total fat 2.5g, saturated fat 0g, trans fat 0g, cholesterol 0mg, sodium 85mg, potassium 70mg, total carbohydrate 2g, dietary fiber 0g, sugars 1g, protein 3g, phosphorus 45mg

Fresh Herb Dip

It's practically a must to have raw vegetables and dip available at any large gathering of family or friends. Serve a real dip that everyone can enjoy freely, like this one. Luckily, this recipe is low in "bad" fats and high in flavor. Plus, enjoying dip along with vegetables has the delicious ability to boost veggie intake.

1 cup low-fat cottage cheese

1/2 cup fat-free plain greek yogurt or organic low-fat sour cream

1/4 cup organic or non-GMO mayonnaise

2 large cloves garlic, minced

1 large shallot, minced

1/4 cup finely chopped fresh flat-leaf parsley

1/4 cup minced fresh chives

1/2 teaspoon vegetarian worcestershire sauce

1/4 teaspoon sea salt

1/4 teaspoon hot pepper sauce

DIRECTIONS

Stir all ingredients together in a large bowl and serve.

Choices/Exchanges: 1/2 lean protein, 1 fat
Per Serving: calories 70, calories from fat 40, total fat 4.5g, saturated fat 1g, trans fat 0g, cholesterol 5mg, sodium 190mg, potassium 65mg, total carbohydrate 2g, dietary fiber 0g, sugars 1g, protein 4g, phosphorus 50mg

FOOD FLAIR

Refrigerate this dip at least 1 hour prior to serving to let flavors mingle. For added flavor interest, stir in 1/8 teaspoon freshly grated or ground nutmeg before serving. Serve with a variety of colorful crudités, such as carrots, cauliflower, cherry tomatoes, broccoli, and/or sweet bell peppers.

MORE THAN FOUR?

When plating this entire recipe for a party, serve it with 10–12 cups of crudités—that's roughly 1 cup of raw veggies per serving of dip.

Party Spinach Dip

Spinach dip that's traditionally made with packaged vegetable soup mix often shows up on casual party buffets. Though tasty, it's loaded with sodium and artificial ingredients. Now you can serve and savor this popular party dip with 100% real ingredients and great taste. Pair it with whole-grain rye bread pieces or seasonal veggies. It'll delight you and your guests.

1 (10-ounce) package frozen chopped spinach, thawed

1 cup fat-free plain greek yogurt or organic low-fat sour cream

1/2 cup organic or non-GMO mayonnaise

1 (8-ounce) can sliced water chestnuts, drained and thinly sliced into match-stick-size strips

4 scallions, green and white parts, thinly sliced

1/4 cup grated carrots

1 large clove garlic, minced

3/4 teaspoon sea salt

1/4 teaspoon hot pepper sauce

1/8 teaspoon freshly grated or ground nutmeg

Serves: 16 | Serving Size: 3 tablespoons
Prep Time: 15 minutes | Cooking Time: 0 minutes

DIRECTIONS

1. Over a small bowl, squeeze the spinach in a double layer of plain, unbleached paper towels until thoroughly dry. Reserve the liquid for another purpose (such as part of the broth for making soup or rice).

2. Combine all ingredients in a medium bowl and serve.

Choices/Exchanges: 1 vegetable, 1 fat
Per Serving: calories 70, calories from fat 50, total fat 6g, saturated fat 1g, trans fat 0g, cholesterol 5mg, sodium 180mg, potassium 105mg, total carbohydrate 4g, dietary fiber 1g, sugars 1g, protein 2g, phosphorus 35mg

FRESH FACT

Dips are definitely fun party fare. They're ideal for special gatherings because you can make most of them, including this spinach dip, in advance. Dips made ahead of time are usually tastier because all the flavors have blended. So make this recipe 1 day before a soirée and keep chilled until near serving time.

MORE THAN FOUR?

Serve this dip with style in a hollowed-out pumpernickel bread boule. Cut or tear out pieces from the center of the loaf before you fill it with dip. Or place a dollop of dip on top of mini rye or sprouted whole-grain bread slices to make "Spinach Dip Bruschetta."

Classic Guacamole with Tomato

Avocados are high in the "good" kind of fat—mostly monounsaturated. And they provide a wealth of heart-protective, plant-based nutrients, including potassium, vitamin E, and folate. What's more, avocados act like nutrient boosters, helping the body absorb more fat-soluble nutrients from the foods you eat with them. So whatever you enjoy this guacamole with will be better for you, too. Try it in Tex-Mex Layer Dip (page 62) and Baja Bean Chili with Guacamole (page 196) or simply serve with organic, baked yellow or blue corn tortilla chips.

2 Hass avocados, peeled, pitted, and cubed

Juice of 1/2 lime (1 tablespoon)

1 medium vine-ripened tomato, seeded and finely diced

1/4 cup finely chopped red or white onion

2 tablespoons chopped fresh cilantro

1 small jalapeño pepper with some seeds, minced

1/4 teaspoon sea salt

DIRECTIONS

Gently stir together all ingredients in a medium bowl until just combined and serve.

Choices/Exchanges: 1 fat
Per Serving: calories 50, calories from fat 35, total fat 4g, saturated fat 0.5g, trans fat 0g, cholesterol 0mg, sodium 60mg, potassium 180mg, total carbohydrate 3g, dietary fiber 2g, sugars 1g, protein 1g, phosphorus 20mg

FRESH FACT

Avocados are good for the environment. Like all tree orchards, avocado orchards help keep the air fresh by producing oxygen and absorbing carbon dioxide. Just one California avocado tree can absorb the same amount of carbon dioxide each year produced by a car driven about 26,000 miles. A couple of mature avocado trees can provide enough oxygen for an entire family.

Fig Guacamole

This chunky guacamole is not any ordinary guacamole. It has figs in it! Throughout the summer and beyond, there are so many delicious varieties of fresh figs to be found, such as Black Mission, Calimyrna, Brown Turkey, and Kadota. If you find them in your area, try the various types in this guacamole recipe for extra enticement. You might find this fruity, yet spicy, figgy guacamole is better than the original. Scoop it up with baked blue corn tortilla chips to enjoy one palate-pleasing bite at a time.

2 Hass avocados, peeled, pitted, and cubed

Juice of 1 lime (2 tablespoons)

3 fresh black mission figs, diced OR 2 dried figs, finely diced

1/4 cup finely chopped red onion

1 small jalapeño pepper with seeds, minced

2 tablespoons finely chopped fresh cilantro

1 clove garlic, minced (optional)

1/2 teaspoon sea salt

1/8 teaspoon ground cumin or coriander

DIRECTIONS

Gently stir together all ingredients in a medium bowl until just combined and serve.

Choices/Exchanges: 1 fat
Per Serving: calories 50, calories from fat 30, total fat 3.5g, saturated fat 0g, trans fat 0g, cholesterol 0mg, sodium 100mg, potassium 155mg, total carbohydrate 5g, dietary fiber 2g, sugars 2g, protein 1g, phosphorus 15mg

FAST FIX

How do you easily prep an avocado? One way is to slice an avocado from top to bottom, all the way around, until you hit the seed. Twist the avocado to form two halves. Hold the seed-containing half in one hand or place it on the counter and firmly, yet carefully, wedge the knife blade into the seed. Twist the knife to remove the seed. With a large spoon, scoop out the avocado as close to the skin as possible.

FOOD FLAIR

Halve the fresh figs, spritz with cooking spray, grill until rich grill marks form, and then dice before adding to this guacamole. The grilled fig version is especially divine.

Salsa Fresca

On a Mexican menu, you might see this salsa called "pico de gallo" or "salsa Mexicana." But whatever you decide to call it, the most important thing is to eat it. Go beyond simply serving with tortilla chips; try it as a delightful topping for poultry, fish, or eggs. The jarred variety won't seem as enticing after enjoying this easy, fresh salsa.

2 medium vine-ripened tomatoes, seeded and diced

1 serrano pepper with some seeds, minced

1 small white onion, diced

1 tablespoon finely chopped fresh cilantro

Juice of 1/2 lime (1 tablespoon)

1/2 teaspoon sea salt

DIRECTIONS

Stir together all ingredients in a medium bowl, and serve.

> **Choices/Exchanges**: free food
> Per Serving: calories 10, calories from fat 0, total fat 0g, saturated fat 0g, trans fat 0g, cholesterol 0mg, sodium 150mg, potassium 80mg, total carbohydrate 2g, dietary fiber 1g, sugars 1g, protein 0g, phosphorus 10mg

FRESH FACT

Salsa is a Latin American dance. It's also the Spanish word for sauce. When referring to the type of salsa you eat, there are plenty of varieties to enjoy: picante (spicy), verde (green), and fresca (fresh)—just to name a few.

Salsa Verde

That bottle of red salsa in your refrigerator will be green with envy when you whip up this recipe! Try this tasty salsa in Blanco Huevos Rancheros (page 30) or California Avocado-Bean Salad with Salsa Verde (page 164). It's equally delicious paired simply with organic baked tortilla chips. In fact, you might find yourself enjoying this green salsa more often than the traditional red.

8 ounces tomatillos, husks removed and rinsed (6–8 tomatillos)

1/4 cup loosely packed cilantro leaves

1 slice of medium white onion

1 large clove garlic

1/8 teaspoon sea salt

Juice of 1/2 lime (1 tablespoon)

Serves: 4 | Serving Size: 1/4 cup
Prep Time: 10 minutes | Cooking Time: 20 minutes

DIRECTIONS

1. Place whole tomatillos in a large saucepan and fill with enough water to cover. Bring to a boil over high heat, then reduce heat to low and simmer until tomatillos are softened, about 10 minutes.

2. Drain and chop the tomatillos. Purée half of them, along with the cilantro, onion, and garlic, in a blender until smooth.

3. Return the purée to the saucepan and add the remaining chopped tomatillos. Cook over medium-low heat until fully heated, stirring occasionally, about 5 minutes. Add the salt and lime juice. Serve at room temperature.

Choices/Exchanges: 1 vegetable
Per Serving: calories 25, calories from fat 5, total fat 0.5g, saturated fat 0g, trans fat 0g, cholesterol 0mg, sodium 75mg, potassium 180mg, total carbohydrate 5g, dietary fiber 1g, sugars 3g, protein 1g, phosphorus 25mg

FRESH FACT

Tomatillos look like small green tomatoes wrapped in papery husks, but they're not tomatoes at all. Rather, these acidic fruits are relatives of gooseberries.

MORE THAN FOUR?

Salsa is party-friendly fare. Serve chips along with two kinds of salsa: a red tomato-based one and this green tomatillo-based one. The red and green colors are especially festive during the winter holiday season.

Bell Pepper–Avocado "Crème" Sauce

Enjoy this antioxidant-rich, vivid orange, velvety smooth sauce with burritos. Or use it like gravy over chicken, brown rice, or grilled vegetables to add flavor and visual pizzazz. Try it as a sandwich spread instead of mayo or mustard, too. It's surprisingly versatile and oh-so-tasty.

2 teaspoons grapeseed or extra-virgin olive oil

3 large red bell peppers, chopped

1 small jalapeño pepper with seeds, chopped

1 small or 1/2 large red onion, chopped

1 Hass avocado, peeled, pitted, and cubed

Juice of 2 limes (1/4 cup)

1/4 teaspoon sea salt

Serves: 12 | Serving Size: 1/4 cup
Prep Time: 18 minutes | Cooking Time: 14 minutes

DIRECTIONS

1. Heat the oil in a large nonstick skillet over medium-high heat. Add the red peppers, jalapeño, and onion and sauté until softened, about 12 minutes. Remove from heat, cover, and let stand to steam and further soften, about 5 minutes.

2. Purée the pepper mixture, avocado, lime juice, and salt in a blender until velvety smooth. Serve warm or at room temperature.

Choices/Exchanges: 1 vegetable, 1/2 fat
Per Serving: calories 40, calories from fat 25, total fat 2.5g, saturated fat 0g, trans fat 0g, cholesterol 0mg, sodium 50mg, potassium 160mg, total carbohydrate 4g, dietary fiber 2g, sugars 2g, protein 1g, phosphorus 20mg

FOOD FLAIR

Make this recipe your own. For a smokier flavor, cook the peppers and onion over medium-high heat for 5 minutes, then over high heat until peppers are slightly blackened, about 5–7 minutes. Alternatively, grill the peppers and onion. The blackened parts of the peppers will add dark flecks of rich, smoky goodness to the sauce. For more spiciness, use a whole, large jalapeño pepper— or just add hot sauce to taste. For a milder version, remove the seeds from the jalapeño.

Balsamic-Basil Tofunnaise

*Are your taste buds ready to be wowed? Here's a zingy basil "mayo."
Use it just like regular mayo—it's a less caloric yet more sensational
condiment for burgers or sandwiches. It's especially good with grilled
artichoke hearts, too.*

4 ounces organic silken tofu, drained (1/2 cup)

2 tablespoons white balsamic or aged balsamic vinegar

12 large fresh basil leaves

2 tablespoons pine nuts, raw or pan-toasted

1 large clove garlic

DIRECTIONS

Purée all ingredients in a blender until smooth, and serve.

Choices/Exchanges: 1/2 fat

Per Serving: calories 25, calories from fat 20, total fat 2g, saturated fat 0g, trans fat 0g, cholesterol 0mg, sodium 0mg, potassium 40mg, total carbohydrate 1g, dietary fiber 0g, sugars 1g, protein 1g, phosphorus 20mg

FAST FIX

Prepare this tofunnaise on Sunday evening and store it, tightly covered, in the refrigerator for up to 5 days. Then it'll be ready at a moment's notice for sandwich fixing every day of the work (or school) week!

Cool Thai Peanut Sauce

Here's a pow for your palate. Though highly flavored, this is a multipurpose sauce. It can be a dipping sauce for chicken fingers or a satay-style sauce with chicken kebabs. It's also inviting tossed with whole-grain or bean-based noodles for a cool salad.

1/3 cup brown rice vinegar

1/4 cup natural creamy peanut butter

Juice of 1 lime (2 tablespoons)

1 tablespoon toasted sesame oil

1 tablespoon naturally brewed reduced-sodium soy sauce

1 tablespoon grated fresh gingerroot

1 tablespoon honey or coconut nectar

1 large clove garlic, chopped

1/4 teaspoon hot pepper sauce

Serves: 8 | Serving Size: 2 tablespoons
Prep Time: 10 minutes | Cooking Time: 0 minutes

DIRECTIONS

Purée all ingredients in a blender until smooth, and serve.

Choices/Exchanges: 1/2 carbohydrate, 1 fat
Per Serving: calories 80, calories from fat 50, total fat 6g, saturated fat 1g, trans fat 0g, cholesterol 0mg, sodium 130mg, potassium 65mg, total carbohydrate 6g, dietary fiber 1g, sugars 4g, protein 2g, phosphorus 30mg

FOOD FLAIR

To make cool Thai-style peanut noodles using this sauce, prepare 4 ounces buckwheat soba noodles according to package directions, rinse, and drain well. Toss with 2 teaspoons toasted sesame oil and chill. Toss cool noodles with 1/4 cup of this peanut sauce and garnish with fresh cilantro to make 3 side-dish servings. Alternatively, jazz up the noodles and serve as a salad tossed with fresh bean sprouts, grated carrots, diced cucumber, sliced scallion, and roasted sesame seeds or peanuts.

Scallion Yogurt Spread

Move over, sour cream! Your baked potato has a new protein-rich, calorie-friendly pal. In addition to being delightful dolloped on top of a baked potato, this yogurt spread can be used in many other dishes in lieu of sour cream, such as tacos and burritos. Or spread it into a grilled-vegetable or chicken wrap. It's a refreshing condiment in place of mayo. Or you can mix it with organic or non-GMO mayo to create a naturally lighter spread.

1 cup fat-free plain greek yogurt

1 scallion, green and white parts, minced

1 small clove garlic, minced

1/8 teaspoon sea salt

Serves: 4 | Serving Size: 1/4 cup
Prep Time: 5 minutes | Cooking Time: 0 minutes

DIRECTIONS

In a small bowl, whisk together the yogurt, scallion, garlic, and salt. Serve immediately or store in a sealed container in the refrigerator for up to 1 week.

Choices/Exchanges: 1/2 fat-free milk
Per Serving: calories 35, calories from fat 0, total fat 0g, saturated fat 0g, trans fat 0g, cholesterol 5mg, sodium 95mg, potassium 90mg, total carbohydrate 2g, dietary fiber 0g, sugars 2g, protein 6g, phosphorus 80mg

FRESH FACT

According to research conducted at the University of Cambridge, eating yogurt regularly may reduce the risk of developing type 2 diabetes by 28% compared to people who don't consume yogurt.

Small Plates and Snacks

Tropical Shrimp Cocktail

Savor this sexy shrimp cocktail. It's so much more exciting than traditional shrimp cocktail, especially when served in martini glasses and alongside organic, baked blue or yellow corn tortilla chips. Be sure to squirt the lime onto your shrimp appetizer then toss the peel into your beverage for additional flavor.

1 pound raw fresh large shrimp, shelled, deveined, and tails removed

1/2 cup grape tomatoes, quartered lengthwise

1/3 cup diced jicama

1/3 cup diced Vidalia or other sweet onion

1 large jalapeño pepper with or without seeds, minced

2 tablespoons chopped fresh cilantro

1 recipe Baja Shrimp Cocktail Sauce (see Fresh Fact)

1/2 Hass avocado, peeled, pitted, and diced

1 lime, halved

recipe continues after photos

Green Juice Smoothie 300

Roasted Orange Bell Pepper Soup 180

Spring Asparagus Stir-Fry   288

Romaine Peppercorn-Steak Salad 154

Dill Freekeh and Roasted Carrot Salad 130